Dear Readers,   April

This is obviously history — don't miss the love story — how Nancy & I fell in love in 1948 when we were Juniors at Gettysburg High School

WE GREW UP IN
GETTYSBURG DURING
WWII & THE 40S

Love & Showers of Blessings,

Bruce

PS Nancy passed away in 2021 after a 73 love affair..., to be continued.

WE GREW UP IN GETTYSBURG DURING WWII & THE 40S

BY

BRUCE AND NANCY WESTERDAHL

EDITED BY

STEVEN W. WESTERDAHL

IBSN: 9798511618791

TABLE OF CONTENTS

INTRODUCTION

During World War II, the town of Gettysburg and the adjacent National Park were very different than they were before 1941 and after 1945. For example, in the first year of the war, tourism dropped by 80% and at times when we hiked or biked the Battlefield, we saw no one.

Gas rationing and a national speed limit of 35 miles per hour, enacted to conserve gas, tires and car parts, were responsible for the loss of tourism. Motels, restaurants and bars that depended on visitors to the area suffered badly during the war years.

That doesn't mean Gettysburg was devoid of traffic. Nancy lived on Baltimore Street on Route 15, and she was often reminded of the war as convoys of trucks carrying troops and supplies rumbled past her house day and night.

Victory gardens were a common sight everywhere in Gettysburg during WWII. Encouraged by the federal government to help prevent a food shortage and to ensure adequate food for our military, residents responded enthusiastically to the request to grow their own food.

Scattered throughout the town were numerous car dealers whose show windows only featured used cars until the end of the war. No new cars were available in Gettysburg until March of 1946 when the new DeSoto Deluxe was on display at Phiel's Garage on York Street.

If you were able to visit Gettysburg in 1944, you might have discovered a tent camp for 500 German prisoners of war on the Battlefield. The camp served as one of many reminders of our country's participation in WWII.

With the end of the war in 1945, life in Gettysburg gradually returned to normal. Soldiers came home, war-time restrictions were lifted and store shelves and auto dealerships were once again fully stocked.

The most significant event of the Forties was obviously World War II, but the decade is also very special to Nancy and me because it is when we fell in love. Growing Up in Gettysburg During WWII reveals how our relationship began in 1948 and has continued for over seventy years.

Bruce and Nancy Westerdahl

DISCOVERING THE BATTLEFIELD

The Gettysburg National Military Park was our nature preserve to explore and our wilderness to adventure in when Nancy and I were growing up in the small Pennsylvania town that became famous throughout the world. From the time we were children, sites like Culp's Hill, Spangler's Spring and Devil's Den were destinations to discover and probe alone or with friends.

My family moved to Gettysburg in 1942 when I was in sixth grade. Our first home was on East Middle Street just a few hundred yards from the entrance to East Confederate Avenue on the Battlefield. That road led to a series of small streams spanned by what we called First Bridge, Second Bridge and Third Bridge. The latter is at the base of Culp's Hill, scene of fierce fighting on July 2-3, 1863.

My earliest recollection of playing on the Battlefield was in the boulders near Third Bridge. There, my neighbor Johnny Aughinbaugh and I gathered dead tree trunks and laid them over the boulders that were about six feet apart and four feet high. Then we piled brush and leaves over the trees, and we completed the coolest "fort" from which to hide from our imaginary enemy. I can remember Mom preparing sandwiches and Kool-Aid for us so we could retire to our fort well supplied.

A few years later, our Boy Scout Troop 77 (Bound for Heaven) played Capture the Flag in the field across from our fort. The spirited, rough and tumble of that game probably helped prepare me for eight years of high school and college football.

Another memory of the Third Bridge area was a field of tall grass northwest of the stream. After exploring that field one day by myself, I returned home covered with what we called "chiggers." It reminded me that hot weather, artillery and rifle fire were not the only concerns both the Union and Confederate soldiers faced during the famous battle.

EAST CEMETERY HILL

When Nancy was in third grade in Gettysburg, her family moved to a house on the east side of Baltimore Street at the base of Cemetery Hill. It was a two story, brick home which may have been standing during the Battle of Gettysburg.

If Nancy had lived there on July 1, 1863, she probably would have been hiding in the cellar with family members. In the late afternoon that day, Union troops were retreating south on Baltimore Street to Cemetery Hill under heavy fire from the Confederates.

If Nancy had lived in that home on November 19, 1863, she would have seen President Abraham Lincoln and local dignitaries up close and personal on their way to the National Cemetery.

When Nancy and I were growing up in Gettysburg in the Forties, a feature attraction on East Cemetery Hill was a huge round brick building called the "Battle of Gettysburg" Cyclorama. Inside, visitors were surrounded by a 377-foot-long painting depicting in spectacular realism the chaos of battle during Pickett's Charge.

The Cyclorama was brought to Gettysburg in 1913 for the celebration of the Fiftieth Anniversary of the Battle. It is now located in the National Military Park Museum and Visitor Center.

On East Cemetery Hill, about 400 yards from Nancy's house on Baltimore Street, there was a monument for Union General Oliver Howard who looked out over the steepest and best hill for sledding in Gettysburg. When the snow fell in the winter, Nancy and her friends spent many hours enjoying that hill which was the scene of fierce fighting in July of 1863.

Photo courtesy of Gettysburg National Park
The Cyclorama on East Cemetery Hill

The sled ride from the top of the hill ended on Wainwright Avenue which led north to our high school and south to Culp's Hill. In the spring the road on the east side was lined with fragrant blossoms of honeysuckle.

SIXTH GRADE AT LINCOLN SCHOOL

When my family moved to Gettysburg from Hanover in 1942, I was enrolled in the sixth grade at Lincoln School, a two-story brick building and former high school which stood at the junction of York and Hanover Streets. Sadly for Lincoln School graduates, it was demolished in 1969.

This was 1942-1943, and World War II was raging in Europe and the South Pacific. A newspaper column called *With our Servicemen* reminded everyone WWII wasn't just a headline. The war was personal, and each week we learned the names of our local men and women who were in basic training or being transferred from one base to another throughout the world.

To finance the war, the government initiated a national defense bond program, offering baby bonds selling for as little as $18.75 which paid $25 in ten years. Lincoln School students enthusiastically supported the bond program by purchasing 10 cent saving stamps each week in their homerooms and placing them in a stamp book until they had accumulated enough to exchange for a bond.

The school was just a little over a block from my house, so I went home every day for lunch. When I arrived, the radio was playing the Kate Smith show featuring her own popular songs and guest stars of that era like Al Jolson, Jackie Gleason and Dorothy Lamour. It was Kate Smith who introduced *God Bless America* on her radio show in 1938.

After lunch, if I had time before school started again, I would stop at Sherman's Grocery Store across from the school. Before large supermarkets, "Mom & Pop" stores could be found within easy walking distance of most homes. At Sherman's, we bought bread, milk, a wedge of cheddar carved from a huge wheel that sat on the counter, butter in bulk or for a treat, penny candy, a popsicle or a bottle of Coke.

After school, I went home, changed clothes and when the weather permitted, played football, basketball or softball with friends in the neighborhood.

SEVENTH GRADE AT LINCOLN SCHOOL

Nancy and I entered Seventh Grade in Lincoln School in Gettysburg in the fall of 1943. In December of 1941, the Japanese attacked Pearl Harbor, and the US declared war on the axis powers of Japan, Germany and Italy.

The students at Lincoln School were enthusiastically involved in the War Effort. Each week, we bought Government Saving Stamps which ultimately, were converted to bonds to help purchase everything the military needed to fight the war, and we collected mountains of tin cans, aluminum foil, lard, milkweed pods for lifejackets and metal for guns and tanks.

Nationwide rationing gas began almost immediately, and depending on how your car was used, a family might only be allowed as little as four gallons a week. Food was also limited and each family was provided with ration stamps to use when purchasing meat and groceries. Many families, including Nancy's, grew their own vegetables in small plots called Victory Gardens.

The War prompted a groundswell of patriotism expressed in songs like *Remember Pearl Harbor* and *Praise the Lord and Pass the Ammunition*. We also listened to the big band sounds of Glenn Miller and Tommy Dorsey on our radios and on 78 rpm records.

Although we eagerly supported the war effort, those of us attending Seventh Grade in Lincoln School were still just kids. During school we participated in organized sports, and after school, we rode our bikes everywhere, played with friends,

7

listened to the radio, and on weekends went to movies and attended church.

Seventh grade was significant for Nancy and me because it was the first year we passed to different rooms for classes, and I specifically remember passing through Mr. Bream's Geography Class and noticing Nancy, a pretty girl with dark hair wearing a different novelty pin every day. Little did we know then that many years later we would celebrate our sixty-eighth wedding anniversary.

EXPLORING THE BATTLEFIELD

The Gettysburg National Military Park which was simply called the "Battlefield" in the Forties when we were growing up in the small town made famous in 1863, was ours to explore and enjoy.

Photo Courtesy of the Library of Congress
Spangler's Spring

General Meade's Headquarters between Hancock Avenue and the Taneytown Road was an easy one-mile bike ride from Nancy's home on Baltimore Street. Today, it is locked and secured, but back in the Forties it was open, and Nancy remembers how frightened she was to explore the dark, damp basement of that little house with friends when she was young.

According to one source, there are 26 miles of paved road on the Battlefield. Over the years, Nancy and I have biked and/or hiked just about every mile alone, together or with other friends. When I was a Boy Scout, we were required to do a 14-mile hike to qualify for a First-Class rank, and Bill Snyder and I walked just about every one of our 14 miles on the Battlefield.

As a Boy Scout, I also remember a weekend when our Troop 77 camped on Pardee Field, a small grassy meadow south of Spangler's Spring. Just over 80 years after fierce fighting on that field, members of our Troop put up pup tents, got water from the spring, cooked on wood fires and told ghost stories around the fire at night. Today the Spring is closed.

The towers on the Battlefield provided excellent sites for Boy Scouts to practice relaying messages using Flag Semaphore during the day or Morse Code with lanterns at night. People are not permitted to be on the Battlefield after dark now, but in the Forties, that was no problem.

Growing up in Gettysburg was a wonderful experience, and as we recall other adventures from our past, we'll be sharing them with our readers.

THE FAMOUS ELECTRIC MAP

One of the main attractions in the famous town where Nancy and I grew up was the Gettysburg National Museum. It was the first place we took friends and family who were interested in learning about the historic battle, because it was the home of the famous Electric Map.

The 900 square foot, 12-ton terrain map was created by Joe Rosensteel in 1939. It was viewed from tiered seating which gave visitors an excellent view of how the three-day battle evolved.

While narrating the events that occurred during the battle, Rosensteel operated a switchboard which activated over 600 colored lights showing the positions of Union and Confederate Armies as they developed.

The walls of the Museum were lined with artifacts from the battle, and bullets, allegedly found on the Battlefield, were sold in the souvenir shop where Nancy worked during summer vacations from college.

When Nancy's father created the family Victory Garden during World War II, Nancy found several bullets from the battle. I looked for artifacts in our family garden on East Middle Street, but apparently, no one shot in that direction on July 1, 2 and 3 of 1863.

Renovations to the original map were made in the 60's, and in 1963 the Museum was sold to the National Park Service. When the new Gettysburg Museum and Visitor Center opened on the Baltimore Pike in 2008, Scott Roland of Hanover paid $14,000 for the unique map which is displayed in that nearby town. In 2009, the building which housed the famous Electric Map was demolished, and the popular Gettysburg attraction was lost. Fortunately, it remains a vivid memory.

75TH ANNIVERSARY OF THE BATTLE OF GETTYSBURG

We Grew Up in Gettysburg during WWII was initially intended to be limited to the years after I moved to that famous historic town in 1942, but Nancy was born there, and she witnessed an event in 1938 when she was seven that deserves to be mentioned here.

Thousands of visitors from all over the country came to Gettysburg from June 29 to July 6, 1938 in observance of the 75th anniversary of the battle which occurred in the historic town in 1863. For five of those days, Gettysburg was declared the official seat of the Pennsylvania government.

Among those in attendance were 1,500 Union veterans and 500 Confederate veterans, honored guests of the state and national governments. Visitors were able to meet and greet the veterans in their Anniversary Camp set up on the Emmitsburg Road.

The program for the eight-day observance included lectures, parades, fireworks, a 48-plane air show, religious services and daily concerts by the U.S. Army Band, but the featured event was the dedication of the Eternal Light Peace Memorial, and the primary speaker was President Franklin D. Roosevelt.

Nancy remembers going with her father to the dedication, but she doesn't recall seeing the President. Our classmate, Bill Snyder, however, has a vivid memory of sitting on his father's shoulders and catching a glimpse of FDR in his Cadillac convertible with a Cavalry escort.

When the Peace Light was dedicated, it was intended that the flame should burn forever, but just a few months after World War II began in 1941, the visible flame was discontinued at night at the suggestion of the local defense authorities. The invisible pilot light continued to burn until the war was over when the visible flame burned 24 hours a day again.

NOTE: Film clips of the 75th Anniversary of the Battle of Gettysburg are available on YouTube.

SUPPORTING THE WAR EFFORT

In the fall of 1943, nearly 4 million men and women of the United States Armed Forces were deployed in Europe and the South Pacific as the fighting in World War II escalated.

Nancy and I and our classmates at Lincoln school in Gettysburg were supporting the war effort in numerous ways. For example, during October and November of '43, students set school records for War Bonds and Stamps sales totaling $1,890.50. During a Bond Drive the following March, our students raised $6,556.70.

In March of 1943, students at Lincoln School collected 28,903 tin cans for the war effort, more than any school in Adams County. We also collected rags, paper, rubber, scrap metal, aluminum foil and milkweed pods. At home we saved bacon grease. The glycerin in recycled fat was used to make ammunition and some medicines.

When an air raid siren sounded during school, Nancy and I remember leaving our classrooms and going out into the inner hallways, sitting on the floor and putting our hands over our heads.

When the air raid siren was heard at night, no light could be seen from any part of our houses. Nancy's father was an Air Raid Warden during the war, responsible for checking every home in his sector in Gettysburg during a drill.

Betty Weiland, the wife of a classmate who lived in the country during the war wrote that she lived on a farm, and they were also required to turn off lights until the all-clear was sounded.

World War II impacted our lives in many ways, and the question asked regularly in movie shorts, posters, radio and in our schools was, "Are you doing everything you can?" I like to think we tried our best.

GOVERNORS VISIT GETTYSBURG ON MEMORIAL DAY 1944

Memorial Day in 1944 was the biggest happening in Gettysburg since Lincoln spoke at the National Cemetery in November of 1863. An estimated crowd of 11,000 including governors from 37 states attended the annual event.

The most photographed man that day was Thomas E. Dewey, Governor of New York and leading candidate for the Republican presidential nomination.

Nancy and I were Seventh Graders, and I was a Boy Scout assigned to a position on the square probably to assist the police in crowd control during the Parade. As the governors passed by on their way to the National Cemetery, Governor Dewey's car stopped just in front of where I was standing.

The window on his car was open and when he extended his hand toward me, I responded with a good firm Boy Scout handshake.

Almost a thousand children from Lincoln, Meade and High Street Schools participated in the Parade that day. Each child carried an armful of flowers which were carefully placed on the headstones in the Cemetery. According to reports, the governors were visibly impressed. Some called the sight inspiring.

That afternoon, the governors and a huge crowd attended the formal program in the Cemetery which was broadcast on 200 radio stations across the country.

While governors, school children, residents and visitors observed Memorial Day in Gettysburg, a headline in the local paper the next day reported that British troops were only 17 miles from Rome as World War II continued in Europe.

GETTYSBURG AND WORLD WAR II

The United States involvement in World War II began December 7, 1941 and ended with the Japanese surrender on September 2, 1945.

Though it was fought thousands of miles from Gettysburg, its effects were quite apparent in our hometown, even for junior high classmates like Nancy and me.

Everyone had a relative or friend in the service. Nancy had a cousin and an uncle fighting Nazi Germany, and I had an uncle fighting the Japanese in the South Pacific. My dad was also called to serve in the Seabees, but he remained in the States.

The July 3, 1944 issue of the *Gettysburg Times* included an Independence Day Tribute honoring the more than 3,100 men and women from Adams County who were in the service in World War II. A headline in that edition reported that, "At least 20 Adams Countians Have Made the 'Supreme Sacrifice." Another headline noted that several others were Prisoners of War in Japan and Germany.

Food and fuel rationing during the war had a negative impact on everyone in Gettysburg especially those businesses that depended on tourists. Nancy and I remember when we rode our bikes on the Battlefield during the War, it was often devoid of traffic.

Life was not the same for residents of Gettysburg as it was before the War, but our sacrifices were insignificant compared to those who served in the Armed Forces far from home.

NEW TEENAGERS AND THE TEEN CANTEEN

When Nancy and I were in seventh grade in Gettysburg in the Forties, a popular place to go to meet friends, dance, and play games on a Saturday night was the Teen Canteen. There were several locations over the years, but the one we remember best was in the first block on the east side of Baltimore Street.

As a new teenager in 1944, dancing to recorded music at the Canteen was an intimidating experience, not just for me but all boys my age.

Typically, I stood awkwardly with my friends on one side of the dance floor and watched while Nancy and the girls danced with each other.

Rarely, were the boys brave enough to invite a girl on to the dance floor.

I hoped to gain some confidence when Sissy Sherman, a neighbor who was in high school, gave me some private lessons. While Sissy taught me how to hold a girl and how to lead her, she never did anything for my courage. As a result when I visited the Canteen, I just stood around looking self-conscious and stupid like most of the other new teenage boys.

Nancy, on the other hand, danced often at the Canteen with her group of friends and on occasion, with an upper classman.

The years during World War II were part of the big band era, and some of the most popular dance bands in 1943 and 1944 were Glenn Miller, Tommy Dorsey, Vaughn Monroe and Harry James. A few of the top vocalists of the age were Frank Sinatra, Dinah Shore and Bing Crosby.

When the Canteen closed, we often went to the Sweetland, a local ice cream parlor for a burger, a coke or a sundae ... sometimes all three!

In Nancy's diaries from the Forties, she often described a Saturday night at the Canteen by writing, "I had a swell time." The adjective "swell" was probably the most used word to describe a guy, a girl, a movie or a good time at the Teen Canteen.

CULP'S HILL: PLAYGROUND AND BURIAL GROUND

Where I grew up on East Middle Street in Gettysburg, I could look out my front door and see the rolling hills of farmland owned by Henry Culp during the battle in 1863. On the second and third days of the Battle of Gettysburg, the Culp's house and barn, which were behind Confederate lines, were used as temporary hospitals.

Photo courtesy of the Library of Congress
Culp Farm

A prominent feature of the farm was a hill southwest of the farmhouse which was held by Meade's army each of the three days battle and anchored the right flank of the Union line. When we were growing up in Gettysburg, Nancy and I often hiked the grounds surrounding Culp's Hill.

My earliest participation in team sports in Gettysburg was on a small plot of ground on the Culp farm just across the street from my house. Neighborhood boys would meet there on weekends or after school and play touch football in the fall or softball in the spring. We often played until the streetlights came on or until we were called for dinner.

"Brother against brother" is a phrase often used by historians to describe the division of families in the Civil War, and one example of that slogan involved Henry Culp's nephews, Wesley and his brother William, both natives of Gettysburg. As they grew up together, both brothers explored and hunted on Uncle Henry's property including the woods on Culp's Hill.

In 1858, Wesley's work took him to Shepherdstown, Virginia, and in 1861, he and his friends joined the 2nd Virginia Infantry. Two years later, he returned to Gettysburg with Lee's army and was killed on or near the hill where he had hunted with his bother William.

When the war began, William Culp enlisted in the 87th Pennsylvania Infantry, a regiment in the Union army. William, who considered his brother a traitor, survived the war, and never spoke of him again.

Culp's Hill and the Culp farm property were our playgrounds growing up in Gettysburg. For Wesley Culp, his playground became his burial ground, and his brother became his enemy.

SUMMER OF 1944 IN GETTYSBURG

During the summer between seventh grade and eighth grade at Lincoln School in Gettysburg, Nancy and her parents were doing their part to support the war effort. She often helped her father in their Victory Garden, then worked with her mother to prepare the produce for canning or freezing.

In the Forties, the freezing compartments in refrigerators were small, so people rented large freezers at a local locker and froze their fruits and vegetables for later use. In her diary for 1944, Nancy notes that she and her father picked a bushel of green beans, then she and her mother prepared the beans for the locker.

During the summer of 1944, I earned money thinning peaches for local growers in the early spring, picked sour cherries in June for the Ortanna or Musselman's Canneries, then picked peaches for the growers in August.

On hot summer days, we swam at six-foot deep Jack's Pool where the ad slogan was "A daily dip, that's our tip." Picnics were popular, and both Nancy's family and mine loved to go to Caledonia, Marsh Creek and the Narrows on weekends for picnics and outings.

Our activities in the summer of 1944 were trivial compared to what was happening in World War II. The front pages of our local and city newspapers were filled with news of the success of US and British forces in Italy, the Soviets in Eastern Germany

24

and Army and Marines in the South Pacific. Unfortunately, the victories at the front were always won at a cost.

On August 9, the front page of the Gettysburg Times reported on these Adams County residents killed, wounded or missing in action (MIA): Sgt. John Felix killed in action in France; Archie Feeser killed in South Pacific; Charles Smith wounded in France; Cpl. Merrill Topper wounded in South Pacific; James Harness wounded in Italy; Donald Price MIA in Italy; Eugene Clapper, MIA in France and Private Maurice Small, the oldest of five brothers from Gettysburg in the service, MIA in France.

When World War II ended, well over a million men and women from the United States were killed, wounded or missing in action.

LETTERS FROM THE FRONT TO NANCY

In previous chapters, I wrote that Nancy and I grew up in Gettysburg during World War II, a global event that dominated the front pages of local and city newspapers from 1941 through 1946. Last week, I mentioned, with regret, how the war became personal when Gettysburg residents in the service were reported killed, wounded or missing in action.

The war came home to Nancy in a very special way when she received letters from her uncle, Chaplain John Strevig who began writing to her when he was with US forces in North Africa. In a letter written from Tunisia in 1943, he wrote about his experiences in Africa, specifically Morocco and Casablanca.

In February 1944, Uncle John wrote a long letter to Nancy from "Somewhere in Italy" in which he described the sights and sounds of that country including Mt. Vesuvius. There, Uncle John obtained a small piece of lava which he sent to his niece. We still have that piece of the historic site today.

One brief note from Uncle John was handwritten while he was assigned to the 701st Tank Destroyer Battalion in Italy. It read: "I am on Anzio Beachhead. Plenty 'hot' now- lots of shelling. Not many safe places. Lovingly, Uncle Johnny".

Uncle John survived heavy fighting at Anzio, and he survived until World War II ended in May 1945. After the war, Uncle John was stationed in Germany before returning to the United States where he continued to serve as chaplain at various Army bases until he retired from the service. He ended his career in the ministry serving Lutheran congregations in Pennsylvania churches.

On May 30, 1953, Nancy and I stood before Lt. Colonel John R. Strevig in Trinity Evangelical and Reformed Church in Gettysburg where he participated in the ceremony in which Nancy and I were united in Holy Matrimony.

ANOTHER WAR AT HOME

Nancy's brief entry for September 11 in her 1944 diary revealed that while we were still fighting the axis in World War II, we were also fighting a war against a highly contagious disease growing up in Gettysburg:

"School was supposed to start today but was postponed 'til next Monday because of polio. It should have started last Tuesday."

Poliomyelitis, often called polio or infantile paralysis, was the most feared disease of our childhood, often leaving those who were infected with an inability to function. It was, and still is, a highly contagious disease.

In August of '44, as Nancy and I were preparing to enter eighth grade in Gettysburg, the county medical director delayed school openings and closed our only public swimming pool.

Children were not permitted in public places including the movie theater, stores, church services and Sunday School. At first, it was reported that the ban applied to children under sixteen, but later, medical authorities announced that children who were sixteen must adhere to the restrictions.

The initial school ban in Gettysburg went into effect on August 21, but when no new cases of polio occurred in the County, health authorities lifted the ban and school was to begin on September 11. Then a new case of polio was discovered, and as Nancy's diary indicates, school was postponed again for another week.

Nancy's diary also suggests that she continued to be active, working in the family Victory Garden, playing games and roller skating with friends or riding her bike on the Battlefield.

The polio epidemic peeked in 1952 when 58,000 cases were reported in the United States. Today, polio vaccines developed in the Fifties have eliminated the disease in all but a few countries around the world.

A THIRD WAR IN THE FORTIES

Nancy and I described how World War II and the war against polio touched our daily lives in the famous town where we grew up.

Recently, we remembered another war we fought every summer as long as we could remember. It was the war against mosquitoes.

Our weapon of choice in that war was an insecticide called Flit used in a hand-held device called a Flit gun. Flit was marketed in very successful cartoon ads created by Theodore Seuss Geisel years before he became Dr. Seuss. His ads typically contained the popular catch phrase, "Quick, Henry, the Flit."

In the fall of 1944, we began to hear about a new discovery that promised to wipe out the mosquito, liquidate the household fly, cockroach and bedbug and control some of the worst insects that ruin crops all over the world.

The new remarkable insecticide, which we were told was safe for humans, was called DDT, and a few years later, the town of Gettysburg began to spray it from the air and from trucks on our streets.

Nancy and I remember the warnings to stay inside during the sprayings, and we recall the distinctive odor when the DDT cloud went by our houses.

In 1948, Swiss Chemist, Hermann Muller, was awarded the Nobel Prize in Physiology and Medicine for his discovery of the amazing new insecticide.

Then in 1962, in her book Silent Spring, biologist Rachel Carson presented evidence that DDT killed wildlife and caused cancer in humans. Today, DDT is banned around the world for agricultural use, but limited use is still permitted, with reservations, in countries where deaths due to malaria are significant.

GERMAN POW CAMP IN GETTYSBURG DURING WWII

Before Nancy and I leave the summer of 1944 behind and begin reminiscing about eighth grade in Lincoln School, we should remind readers of a brief era in Gettysburg history that most tourists never knew existed.

Our memories were jogged when we read the entry for July 1 in Nancy's 1944 diary:

"This afternoon, Bill and I played croquet and Monopoly. After supper, Grandpa and I went with Aunt Sara and Betty Ann to see the German Prison Camp. "

The first POW s were sent to Gettysburg in the Spring of 1944 by the War Manpower Commission to help harvest and process fruits and vegetables for the farms, orchards and canneries in the Adams County area.

Initially, fifty Prisoners of War lived in the National Guard Armory, but when the tent camp on the edge of the borough just west of the Emmitsburg Road was completed, it housed nearly 500 prisoners.

The camp on the Emmitsburg Road was strictly a tent camp, so in November of 1944, it was abandoned and prisoners were moved to other areas including 200 who were interned just off West Confederate Avenue at a location previously known as Camp Colt. Captain Dwight David Eisenhower commanded tank corps troops at Camp Colt during the First World War.

32

Photo courtesy of the Library of Congress
German POW Tent Camp

In 1945, a second POW camp was created at Micheaux State Forest between Chambersburg and Carlisle. German Prisoners of War were secretly interrogated there until they were eventually returned to Germany. In June of 1945, 200 Japanese prisoners were assigned to the camp.

Author Barbara Platt wrote a more complete description of the Gettysburg camp in her book, *This Holy Ground*.

BEGINNING EIGHTH GRADE IN 1944

After a delay of two weeks because of concerns about polio in Adams County, Nancy and I finally started eighth grade at Lincoln School in Gettysburg on Monday, September 18, 1944.

World War II continued in Europe and the South Pacific with Allied victories reported in both areas. Residents of Gettysburg were reminded of the war often as convoys of troops moved through the village streets almost daily. We were also reminded of the cost of war when the local papers reported on County residents who were killed or wounded in action.

For Nancy and me, the war was personal as her Uncle John Strevig was an Army Chaplain in Italy, my Uncle Bud Houck was a cook in the South Pacific, and my Dad, Carl Westerdahl, was a Seabee in Gulfport, Mississippi.

Uncle Bud, who died in 1966, is buried in the Gettysburg National Cemetery, and every December Nancy and I, with friends and family members, place a Christmas Wreath on his grave and many others. The annual event is sponsored by the Sgt. Mac Foundation and the National Wreath Project.

Nancy and I didn't really know each other in eighth grade. I do recall seeing her as I passed through her room on the way to English class.

One of her hobbies was collecting novelty pins that she wore on her blouse or sweater. If that was a scheme to get boys to notice her, it worked on me, but no one would have predicted our wedding nine years later.

Nancy's diary often mentions the most popular songs of that year as reported on a radio program called Your Hit Parade. On Saturday, September 9, for example, the number one song was *I'll Be Seeing You* by Bing Crosby. Bing was popular in 1944, but it was a twenty-nine-year-old baritone from Hoboken, New Jersey named Frank Sinatra who had the teenage bobby soxers screaming and swooning in the aisles. Some of the girls in our class were huge Sinatra fans.

The 1994-45 school year began with optimism that we were winning the war, and the 3,100 men and women from Adams County serving around the world would soon be coming back to their friends and families.

NANCY'S FAMILY TIES TO THE CIVIL WAR

By the time my family moved to the Borough of Gettysburg in 1942, I had lived in four other communities including two in North Jersey.

Nancy, however, didn't just grow up in Gettysburg, her family roots there go back to the early 1800's. Our genealogy records suggest that over 150 ancestors preceded her or were her contemporaries in the Gettysburg/ Adams County Area.

Gettysburg is famous because of what happened there in 1863, and Nancy has several family members with ties to the Civil War and at least two who actually lived through the battle.

Nancy's great grandfather, William Alexander Ogden, fought with the 87th Pennsylvania Volunteers and was captured by the Confederates during the Battle of the Wilderness in 1864. He spent the rest of the war in Andersonville Prison.

Nancy's Great Great Uncle, Francis C. Ogden, was a tenant farmer on the Rose Farm during the battle. He planted the crop on the infamous Wheatfield where over 6,000 men were killed or wounded on the second day of the battle.

Francis' son and Nancy's distant cousin, Francis Charles, fought with the Union Army and was killed in the Battle of Locust Grove, Virginia.

Margaret DeGroff Ogden, Nancy's Great Great Grandmother made an American Flag which she hung proudly on the front porch of her Gettysburg home throughout the battle. Thirteen minnie balls and a shell fragment passed through the flag which had 34 stars. The Ogden Flag is now displayed in the Gettysburg College Library.

My only family tie with Gettysburg is Rev. David Eyster, a distant cousin, who founded the Young Ladies Seminary in town. Tillie Pearce, a student at the school in July of 1863, wrote At Gettysburg one of the best accounts by a resident and witness.

Ogden Flag

MORE ABOUT 1944 AND EIGHTH GRADE

Nancy and I have lots of memories from eighth grade at Lincoln School which began September 18 after a two-week delay because a new case of polio was discovered in the County earlier in the month.

Front page news on September 15 announced that World War II was going well for the Allies. US Marine and Army assault forces were converging on Palau and Morotai which General Douglas MacArthur, hero of the war in the South Pacific, called the last stronghold barring our troops from the Philippines.

In Europe, George Patton's Third Army invaded the Nazi stronghold of Nancy, France, and Russian troops were storming into Warsaw, Poland.

According to Nancy's diary, the number one song on the Hit Parade on the radio was *I'll Walk Alone* sung by Dinah Shore. The most popular entertainment media available to us at that time was movies and radio.

TV wasn't available until after the War, and then the first shows we watched were on a small set in the window of Baker's Radio and Television Store on Baltimore Street. Each night, crowds would stand outside the store watching college and professional sports.

Going to the movies was a weekly ritual, and each time a new movie came to town, we were there. The Academy Award for best motion picture in 1944 went to Casablanca with Humphrey

Bogart and Ingrid Bergman. One of the most misquoted lines in the history of movies was spoken by Bergman who asked piano player Sam (Dooley Wilson) to "Play it, Sam. Play 'As Time Goes By.'" Bergman never said, "Play it again, Sam."

Our first science project in eighth grade was a collection of leaves which we dried, identified and placed in an album. Another collection that fall in which every school child in the US participated was gathering milkweed pods used to make life saving jackets and belts for the military. The goal across the country was to gather 1,500,000 pounds of milkweed!

BRUCE'S BRIEF CAREER IN SCOUTING

In the fall of 1944 when Nancy and I were in eighth grade at Lincoln School, the local news reported costly damage to coin operated, viewing machines on the Battlefield. Apparently, in an attempt to recover the dimes used to operate the giant binoculars, the tops of the $700 machines were broken open.

In addition, two monuments were damaged and names were scrawled on others. Vandalism was also reported at Spangler's Spring.

Undoubtedly, it was incidents like this that ultimately led to the National Park closing from dusk until dawn.

When I turned twelve in 1943, I joined Boy Scout Troop 77 at the Methodist Church on East Middle Street. Jack Cessna, the physics teacher at the high school, was the scoutmaster, and he kept us active working for merit badges and camping on the Battlefield and sites throughout Adams County.

My days as a Boy Scout ended the night our scoutmaster took us to a Gettysburg High School football game during a scheduled weekly meeting. Gettysburg was losing the game when our scoutmaster ordered us back to the meeting room. I went AWOL so I could watch the rest of the game, and that was the end of my career in Scouting.

It was late in the season, and only one game remained to be played when Johnny Aughinbaugh and I were invited to practice with the varsity.

40

Subsequently, we were ground down, swallowed up and spit out by linemen fifty to sixty pounds heavier and three or four years older. I still wonder why the coaches thought that was a good idea.

On November 7, of 1944, President Franklin Roosevelt won his fourth term with Senator Harry Truman as his Vice President. The following April, Roosevelt died and a month later, the war with Nazi Germany was over. President Harry Truman would now lead our country in the war against Japan.

GOING UP-STREET IN GETTYSBURG

Everyone who is familiar with Gettysburg remembers that four main streets converge in the center of the village which locals call the "Square." Those of us who grew up in the famous historic town, lived within easy walking distance of that Square, the center of commercial activity.

The square was upstreet for Nancy

When we were in eighth grade at Lincoln School, Nancy lived at the bottom of the Baltimore Street Hill, so she and her friends walked "up-street" to get to the Square. I lived on East Middle Street, and I called the trip going "uptown."

Nancy's diaries from 1944 and 1945 reveal that she went up-street a lot, mostly with friends and most often to eat! Her favorite places were the Delecto and Britcher and Bender on Chambersburg Street, Shuman's on Baltimore Street and the Sweetland on Baltimore Street.

After school, sporting events or the Teen Canteen, teenagers gathered at such places to drink cherry cokes, eat hamburgers or dine on special treats like CMPs (Chocolate, Marshmallow, Peanut) sundaes.

On Friday and Saturday nights, the older high school boys gathered in front of the Sweetland *Watching All the Girls Go By*. Some girls were embarrassed when the boys ogled or whistled but most obviously enjoyed the attention.

Eighth graders weren't driving yet, so out-of-town eateries were not included on our schedules until a few years later. Then we were eager to drive to our out-of-town favorites where we could not only eat but enjoy dancing to jukebox music.

Nancy and I loved growing up in Gettysburg in the Forties, and we make nostalgia trips back to our hometown two or three times each year.

MORE ABOUT EIGHTH GRADE IN 1945

When Nancy and I were in eighth grade at Lincoln School in Gettysburg in 1944-45, our students bought Savings Stamps and War Bonds and collected scrap iron and other materials to make equipment for our troops fighting in World War II in Europe and the South Pacific.

In January of 1945, Lincoln School students won the Adams County Salvage Honors for collecting 12,688 tin cans the previous month. That was 61 cans per student, one of the highest ratios in the State.

Later that month, the *Gettysburg Times* reported that our eighth-grade homerooms bought so many War Bonds, the money raised could buy a walkie-talkie, a pair of binoculars, a blockbuster bomb, a first aid kit and a Jeep!

Also in January a new Youth Center opened on Chambersburg Street for junior high students on Friday evenings from 7 to 10. In a previous post, we noted that at junior high dances, the boys hung out together and watched the girls dance. Rarely did you see boys and girls dancing together.

I started at center on the Lincoln School basketball team in eighth grade, and Nancy was a cheerleader. Basketball was a different game in the Forties. Set shots were made with two hands and foul shots were scooped up from below the waist.

Lincoln School Basketball Team

There was no game clock, and freezing the ball meant fans could take a nap, and the score would be the same when they woke up. Scoring was a reason for celebrating … by fans only. A player who celebrated after scoring would find himself on the bench for the rest of the game. My average of two goals per game was enough to rank me second in scoring for the season.

When the season was over, our captain, Bill Eisenhart, had a party at his house where most of us smoked cigarettes and thought we were cool.

A TRAGEDY IN EIGHTH GRADE

Gene Hertz, or "Hertzy" as his eighth-grade classmates referred to him, was a student at Lincoln School which Nancy and I attended in 1945. Many years earlier, when Nancy lived on Liberty Street in Gettysburg, she and Hertzy were playmates.

On Thursday morning March 8, Nancy and Hertz were in Miss Boyer's study hall class when he got up from his desk in the farthest row from the door, walked across the back of the room, through the door and shot himself in the head in the hall just outside the classroom. The time was 11:15 a.m.

Eugene Hertz did not regain consciousness and died at the Annie Warner Hospital in Gettysburg that same day at 1:05 p.m. He was sixteen.

Over the past seventy years, I have heard several accounts of this shocking incident from fellow classmates who were present in the room. For example, I remember hearing from a few students that Hertz showed the .22 caliber revolver to the class before he left the room. Someone used the phrase "brandished the gun."

At some point, Nancy and others hid under their desks, and just recently, our friend Janet Upton who was in study hall that day, told us that she and other students huddled together in the rear of the classroom.

I remember taking a spelling test in a nearby classroom when the gun went off and my pen moved erratically across the paper when I heard the shot.

After Hertz's death, some students at Lincoln School remembered that Hertz was despondent because his brother and friends were in the military service in World War II, but he was too young to join. They also remember Hertz threatened to commit suicide, but a police investigation following the incident never revealed a reason for the tragedy.

GROWING UP ON BALTIMORE STREET

When we were growing up in Gettysburg in the Forties, Nancy lived on Baltimore Street, one of the most important locations during the three-day battle that occurred in that famous village in 1863.

Baltimore Street and the adjacent Washington Street were the two north/south roads the Union Army used as the battle began, and on which it retreated in the afternoon and evening of the first day. It was also the route that President Lincoln travelled to deliver his famous speech at the new National Cemetery on November 19.

When Nancy walked the .3 of a mile from the town square to her two-story home at the base of the Baltimore Street Hill, she passed numerous sites associated with the battle.

For example, the Presbyterian Church on the corner of Baltimore and East High Street was one of many churches in Gettysburg that served as hospitals during and after the battle. It is also the church President Lincoln attended on the afternoon of his visit to Gettysburg. On February 1, 1963, President and Mrs. Dwight David Eisenhower became members of that church.

As the Union army retreated along Baltimore Street many soldiers hid from the Rebels in houses, basements, attics and sheds of the residents along the way.

48

One home across from Nancy's house, was owned by cabinet maker Henry Garlach, and it was here that Union General Alexander Schimmelfennig hid behind a woodpile. When Nancy was growing up, she remembers that a Garlach family still owned the home.

Another historic building across the street from Nancy's home is the Farnsworth House, which is a restaurant and inn today and known as one of the most haunted houses in America. The Farnsworth House and many of the two-story houses along the street were used by Confederate sharpshooters during the three-day battle.

Living and walking on Baltimore Street in Gettysburg was and still is a history lesson about the most significant battle of the Civil War.

COLLECTING BUTTERFLIES FOR EIGHTH GRADE SCIENCE

Nancy and I remember very little about eighth grade science at Lincoln School when we were growing up in Gettysburg in the Forties. We do recall an assignment that required each student to collect and mount butterflies.

This was 1945, long before people were concerned about protecting endangered animals and insects. Matter of fact, we were enthusiastic about the project and planned to gather as many different species of the colorful insect as possible.

I began the assignment by rounding out a wire coat hanger and taping it to an old broom handle I had shortened. Then I took a large piece of gauze, sewed the sides and stitched it to the coat hanger. I was now prepared to begin the hunt.

The Battlefield, with its large open fields of grass and wildflowers, was the perfect place to begin, and in a few days I collected nine different species to mount and display.

Since eighth grade seventy years ago, I have learned that many others across the country had the same assignment in high school or junior high.

There are now more than two dozen threatened, endangered and extinct butterflies in the United States. Without a doubt, insensitive teachers and eager competitive students, unfortunately, contributed to that reality.

How many butterflies have you seen lately?

GETTYSBURG CELECBRATES VICTORY IN EUROPE DAY

Nancy and I were only one month away from graduating from eighth grade when the front page of the Gettysburg Times reported in huge bold letters the news everyone waited four long years to hear: GERMANY SURRENDERS.

On May 7, 1945, the chief of staff of the German army, General Gustav-Jodl, signed the unconditional surrender, and Admiral Karl Doenitz ordered the capitulation of all German fighting forces.

According to the Times, the people of Gettysburg remained calm as they waited for the official announcements from Washington, London and Moscow. In anticipation of that news from the Allied leaders, Victory in Europe Day services were planned for the following evening at 8:15 on the square.

The following day, photos of Stalin, Churchill and Truman appeared on the front page of the Times which reported the war in Europe was officially over.

That night, several thousand gathered on the square in Gettysburg to hear leading citizens of the community pay tribute to the servicemen and women who helped defeat Germany.

The speakers expressed our joy for the victory, sorrow for those who lost their lives and a rededication of our effort to defeat the Japanese in the West where the war would continue for another four months. Silent prayer was followed by the singing of the *Lord's Prayer* and the *Star-Spangled Banner*.

For Nancy and me and millions of others the continuation of the war with Japan meant our loved ones would not be coming home yet. Not yet!

TELEPHONES AND RECORDS IN THE FORTIES

Growing up in Gettysburg in the Forties, telephone party lines were common. As Nancy and I recall, both our families had four-party lines which meant three other families shared each line with us. Pick the phone up at any time, and you might hear one of your neighbors talking. If you were an eavesdropper, you might hear news that you wouldn't read in the daily newspaper.

Each home on a party line had a specific ringing cadence. For example, your distinctive ring might be two longs and a short and your neighbor might be two shorts and a long. Parents and phone companies asked us to limit our phone calls to five minutes, but Nancy and I remember talking for as long as 30 minutes. When I wanted to call her, I picked up the receiver and if no one was on the line, the operator said, "Number please," and I would answer "29 W."

Vinyl records that played at 78 revolutions per minute were also popular in the Forties and are now only seen on eBay or in antique stores. They were most often played on a portable record player.

Nancy and I enjoyed listening to the popular music of the day, and her diaries from the Forties often mention spending time listening to artists like Kay Kayser, Sammy Kaye, Perry Como, Bing Crosby and of course, Frank Sinatra.

My mother worked at the Bookmart on Chambersburg Street in Gettysburg where records were sold, and a feature of the store was the availability of booths where customers could play a record before deciding if they wanted to buy it.

54

VE DAY AND BEYOND

When victory over Germany was declared on VE Day, May 8, 1945, the Allies were still fighting Japan in the South Pacific. American troops in Europe now began training to be relocated to the Far East.

Local newspapers continued to carry stories of County residents who were missing, wounded and killed in action. On June 8, 1945, for example, the front page of the Gettysburg Times reported that Donald Little and Paul Tate were wounded and Robert Grissinger and Nesbur Brandt were killed.

More men and women would lose their lives as the war continued for more than two months before the Japanese surrendered.

Throughout the war, military units used the hills, fields and forests of the Gettysburg Battlefield for training exercises, and often visiting soldiers were given an understanding of what actions led to victory in the conflict in 1863.

Military convoys passing through Gettysburg were often given space on the Battlefield to rest before moving on to their new duty stations.

In addition to the war news, the June 8 issue of the *Gettysburg Times* also carried a story about 62 students who graduated from Lincoln School, and would enter Gettysburg High School in the fall. Nancy and I were among those who looked forward to our high school careers.

At Lincoln School, we had been "top dogs." Now we would be freshmen, the new kids on the block subject to intimidation and hazing by upperclassmen. On the bright side, we looked forward to new friends and new opportunities in sports, music and other extra-curricular activities.

SUMMER OF '45

After graduation from eighth grade in Lincoln School in the spring of 1945, it was time to look for a summer job. Adams County is home to one of the finest fruit-producing regions in the United States, and there were lots of opportunities to work in the orchards north and west of Gettysburg.

After I thinned peaches for a few weeks, Nancy and I both turned to picking sour cherries, which in the summer of 1945 paid forty cents for an eight-quart bucket. Unfortunately, although we were motivated, neither one of us was very proficient at the job, so our daily wages were minimal.

After cherry picking, Nancy spent the rest of that summer helping her Dad in the Victory Garden, and preparing beans, cherries, peaches and tomatoes for freezing or canning. I went on to work in the kitchen at a church camp in Connecticut until the middle of August.

For entertainment, Nancy and her friends cheered for their favorite softball team, attended movies at the Majestic and the Strand, visited the Teen Canteen on weekends, and drank lots of cokes at the local soda shops.

World War II in Europe was over in June, but the conflict with Japan continued, and many soldiers, sailors and Marines would be casualties before the middle of August when the war finally ended.

The most popular song in the summer of 1945 was *Sentimental Journey* by the Les Brown Orchestra and sung by Doris Day. Nancy and I would dance to that song many times over the coming years, but not in 1945. Not yet!

MORE ABOUT THE SUMMER OF '45

In our most recent post about summer activities in 1945, we referred to our unproductive attempts to earn money by picking cherries That reference prompted a response from our classmate and good friend Bill Snyder. Bill's name must be in the Cherry Picking Hall of Fame for his exploits in the summer of 1947 when he picked 432 quarts of berries in one day.

For that remarkable achievement, Bill earned $17.28 or the equivalent of $1.44 per hour, substantially higher than the average hourly wage in the country in June of 1947 of $1.10 an hour.

Bill also reminded us of one of our favorite summer activities growing up in Gettysburg, swimming. Gettysburg can be very hot in the summer, and low-cost window air conditioners were not available until 1947, so we frequently looked for opportunities to go for a swim.

Jack's Pool was an easy bike ride downhill and south of Gettysburg on the Baltimore Pike. The return trip on our bike was not so easy. Our bikes, like everyone else's in 1945, were single speed bikes, so the ride back up that hill after a swim left us needing another swim to cool off.

If you didn't mind the slugs and snakes, a six-mile bike ride to Marsh Creek Heights, south of Gettysburg on Route 15 was a natural swimming hole and free. Unfortunately, there were many hills on that road but none as steep as the Baltimore Hill.

Caledonia, a half hour west of Gettysburg by car, was a great place to picnic by a mountain stream or swim in a public pool where the water was always beautiful and clear. Laurel Lake at Pine Grove Furnace State Park north of Gettysburg was also a little over a half hour drive. Both Parks are still in use today.

JAPANESE SURRENDER IN AUGUST 1945

Three of the most significant events in American History occurred in August of 1945, just as Nancy and I prepared to enter our freshman year at Gettysburg High School.

On August 6, 1945, President Harry Truman announced that a single bomb, more powerful than 20,000 tons of TNT, was dropped on Hiroshima, Japan. It was an atomic bomb, the most powerful explosive ever used in the history of warfare, and it killed between 70,000 and 80,000 people.

The United States was now in a position to obliterate rapidly and completely every major industrial center in Japan, the nation that had attacked Pearl Harbor without warning on December 7, 1941.

On August 9, three days after the bombing of Hiroshima, the United States dropped a second atomic bomb on the city of Nagasaki, an important port and industrial center.

News of the Japanese surrender arrived in Gettysburg on Tuesday at 7:00 in the evening on August 14, 1945, and the town "went wild." Fire sirens, factory whistles, horns and church bells sounded constantly for over a half hour, and people filled the square talking about the good news.

Nancy and I still have an original copy of the Victory Edition of the *Gettysburg Times* published that day. The good news was reported in three-inch bold face type on the front page. The bad news appeared on page two where it was reported that 118

Adams Countians were killed or died in the service in World War IL Eight were still listed as missing in action. Hundreds were wounded and two county men were still listed as prisoners of the Japanese.

The other good news was more personal. The end of the war meant Nancy's uncle and cousin and my father and uncle would soon be coming home.

FRESHMEN AT GETTYSBURG HIGH SCHOOL

Nancy and I began our freshman year at Gettysburg High School on Tuesday September 4, 1945, a day after Labor Day and less than a month after VJ Day and the end of World War II.

The local paper reported that tourist travel over the battlefield during Labor Day weekend was the largest since 1940 and topped all wartime figures by a huge margin. The National Park Office reported that 11,390 tourists had visited the battlefield that weekend, more than all the visitors that came during all the war years combined.

Nancy and I entered the High School just a block off Baltimore Street, in the approximate location of the current renovated Middle School. The school's front door was less than 100 yards from the backdoor of Nancy's home on Baltimore Street. I lived on East Middle Street, just a four-minute walk from the school. We were fourteen at the time, and though we knew each other well, we wouldn't be dating for another two years.

As we began this next chapter in our lives, we were excited and eager, but often confused moving through the long and unfamiliar halls looking for our next class.

Thanks to the generosity of fellow classmate, Barb Seiferd, Nancy and I have many copies of The Maroon and White, our school newspaper which was so well done and which received many national honors during our four years at GHS. We will refer to the paper often in future posts.

63

The October 10 issue of that paper reported that we had 175 students in our freshman class. Nancy and I were surprised to see that number, because four years later only 140 students were in our graduating class. Sadly more than half the classmates with whom we shared our joys and our successes over four years are deceased.

At the time, we had no thought about building memories that would last a lifetime. We just wanted to find the next class and arrive on time.

CLASS SCHEDULE, SPORTS AND TEEN CANTEEN

On our first day as freshmen at Gettysburg High School in 1945, Nancy and I found our homerooms with no problem, but locating our classrooms for English, Algebra, Biology, Civics and Latin were a bit more difficult. Yes, we took Latin, and we were bored.

When it was time to consider clubs and activities, Nancy was elected to the Student Council and chose to work in the library. She was also very enthusiastic about joining the Girls' Athletic Association, and over the next four years she was very active in basketball, volleyball and field hockey. Unfortunately, there were no interscholastic teams for girls at that time. I played JV football and basketball and won a letter in Varsity track in the spring.

An article that fall in our school newspaper, reviewed the previous two varsity football seasons reporting that the team only won one game.

During that time, they were outscored 409 to 42. We wondered what it would take that year to make the team a winner?

An article in that same paper urged students to "do your bit to give your athletic teams a new name." Unfortunately, Nancy and I were seniors before our teams would no longer be called, "Junior Bullets" or "Little Bullets," names borrowed from the "Bullets" of Gettysburg College.

Outside of school, Nancy and I were socially active with our friends often at the Teen Canteen on Friday and Saturday nights. Opened in 1944 in the YWCA on the square, it was later moved to a vacant building in the first block of Baltimore Street. We slow danced and jitterbugged to the music of Harry James, Les Brown, Johnny Mercer and the other bands of the Swing Era.

HIGH SCHOOL FOOTBALL IN 1945

The fall of 1945 was a time of great anticipation for many families in Gettysburg. World War II was over, and the men and women of Adams County who had served in the military were on their way home. Joyful reunions with loved ones who were apart, sometimes for years, were occurring all over the County that fall.

At Gettysburg High School, students were anticipating another football season. After winning only one game during the past two years, the team was making a fresh start under a new coach, Bill Ridinger, who had an enviable record at Columbia High School.

Those of us who were just beginning to compete in high school football were nervous and excited wondering how we would perform playing the game which in 1945, looked a bit different from what we watch today.

As a freshman, I played Junior Varsity football. We played in hand-me-down uniforms and equipment including unpainted leather helmets with no face guard. Matter of fact, I played football from 1945 through 1951 and never wore a face guard which was only available if you had a broken nose.

Our football jerseys were made of wool, and the pants were a canvas material that hung loosely on our legs. Our shoes were also hand-me-downs from the Varsity, often disfigured from many years of wear.

We played the game on a natural grass field. I still remember the pleasant odor of newly mown grass on a chilly fall evening under the lights.

Sometimes after rain, we played in mud, and when a grass field was frozen, it was like playing on concrete. Artificial turf on a football field was unknown until 1966 when it was installed for the first time in the Astrodome in Houston.

The game was different as well. I didn't experience two-platoon football until I played in college in 1950. All through high school I played offense and defense, and substitutions were rare. Quarterbacks were trusted to call the plays and a no-huddle offense was unknown. Passing was limited.

RATIONING IN WORLD WAR II

A report in the September 9 issue of the *Gettysburg Times* in 1945 announced that World War II shoe rationing could end by October 1. The article reminded us that we have written about the rationing of food during the war, but haven't mentioned more than a dozen other products that were controlled.

Shoes are almost as important to a military machine as food and weapons, and in World War II, the military had a great need for leather for shoes and combat boots. Just two months after the War began, each civilian man, woman and child was limited to three pairs of leather shoes a year.

Two million trucks were manufactured during the War, and they all ran on rubber tires, the very first product to be rationed. The Japanese controlled the rubber producing regions of Southeast Asia, and we did not yet have adequate manufacturing capacity for making synthetic rubber.

To save wear on tires and improve mileage, a nationwide speed limit of 35 mph was enforced on all highways during the War. The reduced speed saved wear on our cars as well, an important consideration since no new cars were manufactured until after the war.

Nylon stockings weren't rationed during the war. There weren't any. All supplies of nylon were essential to the war effort for parachutes, ropes and netting. American female ingenuity met the challenge by carefully applying a makeup liquid that looked like stockings and finished it off with an eyebrow pencil to resemble a seam. Fake nylons only lasted until the real thing was once again available. Thank goodness!

Nancy and I don't remember any specific hardships growing up in Gettysburg during the War. Despite rationing, we had adequate food, clothing and shelter, and any inconveniences we experienced didn't seem to bother us.

SLOW DANCING AND JITTERBUGGING IN 1945-46

When Nancy and I were freshman at Gettysburg High School in 1945-46, one of our favorite activities was dancing with friends to the popular music of the day.

Music for dancing was available from several sources including the radio, the Teen Canteen on Baltimore Street, Woodlawn on the Chambersburg Road or school dances. If we had a favorite song we wanted to play over and over, we bought the 78rpm, 10-inch record for seventy-five cents and played it on our personal record player.

The most popular place to dance on a weekend or a holiday was the Teen Canteen where a juke box usually provided the music. On Labor Day in 1945, one hundred and seven teens showed up and danced to the music of the Junior Jivesters from Gettysburg High School.

Nancy and I danced often at the Teen Canteen, but not in our freshman year. We'll save those stories for another day.

When we started dating as juniors, one of our favorite places to dance was Woodlawn on the Chambersburg Road. A colorful jukebox was available with the most popular music of the day, and each song cost a nickel.

Our favorite bands when we were freshmen were Harry James, Les Brown and Woodie Hermann, and our favorite songs were *Sentimental Journey* for slow dancing and *On the Atchison, Topeka &*

the Santa Fe for jitterbugging. The most popular novelty song was *Chickery Chick*.

Nancy and I don't dance much anymore, but we still listen to the music from our high school days on Big Band jukebox on Live 365 and Forties on Four on Sirius Radio.

HANGIN' OUT AFTER SCHOOL

When Nancy and I were freshmen at Gettysburg High School in 1945, classes were over at 3:30.

After school, Nancy often participated in interclass competition in volleyball, basketball or field hockey. Unfortunately, seventy years ago, there were no interscholastic sports for high school girls.

On days when she had no games or other extra-curricular activities, Nancy would leave school, and go "upstreet" with her girlfriends to Britcher and Bender, Fabers or the Delecto for an afternoon treat.

The most popular place to meet friends after school for treats was the Sweetland on Baltimore Street near the southeast corner of the square.

Every afternoon and evening the booths at the Sweetland were filled with students enjoying sodas, sundaes or cherry cokes.

On Saturday nights, the upper-class guys hung out in front of the Sweetland and watched the girls go by. The boys whistled and the girls giggled.

I played Junior Varsity football as a freshman, so I had practice or games after school, but I still found time to join my friends on weekends.

Varsity football during our freshman year was very discouraging. During the two previous seasons, GHS won only one game, and in the fall of 1945, we lost the first two games by identical scores of 26 - 0. During the same period, our JV team won two of their first three games. There was hope for the future.

We have mentioned before that our teams in 1945-46 were called the Little Bullets, but that was only until our senior year when the Student Council proposed a school vote to change the name. From 1949 until today, teams at GHS have been the Warriors! Nancy and I still consider ourselves Warriors, but now we fight all the problems that go along with aging!

SLANG AND EXPRESSIONS IN THE FORTIES

When Nancy and I were growing up in Gettysburg in the Forties people used words and expressions we don't hear much anymore. For example, when writing in her diary in 1947, Nancy described a boy in her class as "swell." I remember calling a cute girl "a real dish," and a classmate was quoted in the Maroon and White suggesting a boy was "hubba hubba."

Does anyone "neck" anymore? That's what Nancy and I did with our "kissers" in the Forties.

Bud Abbot and Lou Costello were one of the most popular comedy teams of the Forties and Fifties, and if we enjoyed one of their thirty-six movies, we might have told others, "It was a gas." meaning it was funny and we had a good time. We might also tell others that it "Cracked us up!"

Nancy and I are both descended from the Pennsylvania Dutch, and if one of us visited Grandma, and her cookie jar was empty, she would never say, "The cookies are all gone." To her, the cookies were simply "all." Our Grandmas also referred to paper bags as "pokes" or "toots" pronounced like the double oo in "foot."

If one of us got in trouble at Grandma's house, she might scold us saying, "You daresn't do that." That rebuke was sometimes shortened to, "You "dasn't do that." If we thought we were scolded unfairly, we might think to ourselves, "Why is Grandma 'raggin' on me?" We would never actually say that to her.

Expressions of disbelief we haven't heard for many years include "piffle," "fiddlesticks," "horse feathers" and "poppycock." Any one of those words from the past would describe most promises by our politicians in the present.

GETTYSBURG HIGH SCHOOL SPORTS IN THE FORTIES

I played in my first game of football at Gettysburg High School in October of 1945. I didn't start in that game against the Carlisle jayvees, but I came in as a sub and blocked two extra point attempts. That earned a mention in the *Gettysburg Times* and a starting position for the rest of the season and the rest of my football career in high school and college.

In 1945, Gettysburg High School was a member of the South Penn Conference for football, basketball, baseball and track. The other schools in the Conference were Carlisle, Chambersburg, Hanover, Hershey, Mechanicsburg, Shippensburg and Waynes-boro.

While Nancy and I were students at GHS, our teams were competitive in basketball typically winning more games than we lost. In our junior year, we lost to Chambersburg in the Conference Championship game.

As we reported in previous posts, Nancy played intramural field hockey, basketball and volleyball, because unfortunately, there were no opportunities to compete against other high school teams at that time.

Basketball, when Nancy played, involved three girls on offense (forwards) and three on defense (guards) with a mid-court line neither group could cross. All players were only permitted two dribbles each time they handled the ball. Full court, five players basketball was adopted by girls in 1971.

77

Nancy and I are amazed at the level girls play basketball today, and I truly believe a good team now could beat almost any boys' team I played on in high school. Given the size, speed and skills of some of the girls who play basketball now, we wouldn't have an advantage in any area.

GETTYSBURG IS STILL THE SMALL TOWN WE REMEMBER

Nancy and I entered Gettysburg High School in the fall of 1945 when an article in the local paper reported that approximately 16,000 people visited the National Military Park the preceding year. By the time we graduated in 1949, the number of visitors increased to over 43,000, and in 2012, the Gettysburg/ Adams County Chamber of Commerce reported that 1.2 million people toured the historic site.

While visitors to the Park increased dramatically over the years, the number of residents in the borough has not. When Nancy and I were growing up in Gettysburg the population of the town was 7,000. Today, it is 7,600.

The reason the town doesn't grow is because it is surrounded by the Battlefield. The fields and hills where rivers of blood ran freely in 1863 prevent the growth of the town we remember when we were growing up.

Today, there are more tourist shops and restaurants, and the high school and athletic fields where we competed are gone, but many of the streets we travelled are virtually the same. Of course, the Battlefield with a few exceptions is also the same. We hope it will always endure as a shrine to the brave men who fought and died there.

There are also ghosts in Gettysburg now. We don't remember ghosts in the Forties. We suspect they were always there. They just needed someone to look for them, find them and promote them.

NOVELTY SONGS FROM THE TWENTIES AND FORTIES

When I was growing up in Gettysburg in the Forties, my parents had a Victor phonograph that was in my grandparents' house when my Mother was growing up in York, Pennsylvania in the Twenties. The wind up non-electronic acoustical record player held dozens of 78 records which I played over and over because they were so entertaining.

Some of my favorites from the Twenties were the novelty songs like *Crazy Words*, *Crazy Tune* and *Don't Bring Lulu*. Readers can find both these and many other songs of the Twenties on YouTube.

When Nancy and I grew up in Gettysburg in the Forties, we enjoyed a number of novelty songs, sometimes called nonsense songs. Here are a few samples of the lyrics to several which became big hits in the Forties.

One song we remember best was *Mairzy Doats*, which first made the pop charts in 1944 but was featured in movies and television as late as 2000.

"Mairzy doats and dozy doats and fiddle lamzy divey A kiddley divey too, wouldn't you?
Yes! Mairzy doats and dozy doats and fiddle lamzy divey,
A kiddley divey too, wouldn't you?"

Chickery Chick by Sammy Kaye was number one in 1945. I don't remember jitterbugging to the song. Mostly, we just got a kick out of singing the silly lyrics:

"Once there lived a chicken who would say, 'Chick-chick', 'Chick-chick'
all day,
Soon that chick got sick and tired of just 'Chick-chick',
So one morning he started to say,
'Chickery chick, cha-la, cha-la,
Check-a-la romey in a bananika,
Bollika, wollika, can't you see,
Chickery chick is me?'"

The *Hut Sut* song was supposed to be Swedish. It isn't.

"Hut-Sut Rawlson on the Rillerah and a brawla, brawla sooit,
Hut-Sut Rawlson on the Rillerah and a brawla sooit. Hut-Sut Rawlson
on the Rillerah and a brawla, brawla sooit,
Hut-Sut Rawlson on the Rillerah and a brawla sooit."

Wind up Victrola

THE FORTIES LOOK

When Nancy and I were freshmen at Gettysburg High School in 1945, did we look any different than the students entering high school seventy years later in 2015? A check of our 1945-46 yearbook and a trip down memory lane reveals there were definitely differences.

For example, no one wore blue jeans in 1945.

During WWII, blue jeans were declared an essential commodity and were only sold to people who worked in the war industry. Jeans didn't become popular with teens until the Fifties.

In our 1945-46 yearbook, most of the girls are pictured wearing white sox and loafers. It was the traditional footwear for that time, and it resulted in the name bobbysoxer. Bobbysoxers had the reputation of screaming and swooning when they attended a concert by a heartthrob like Frank Sinatra. The yearbook photos also show girls in blouses and knee length skirts. Slacks were never worn to school in the Forties.

The only shoes the boys wore that were different were clodhoppers, large, heavy boots that a few of the boldest guys painted with names of girls, sports teams or movie stars. No one wore sneakers. They were for gym class only.

We don't remember boys wearing shoulder length hair, ponytails, beards or mustaches. Moms and coaches would have objected. Some of us had crew cuts or flat tops. I got my haircut every two weeks at the Varsity Barber Shop on Baltimore Street where the conversation was typically about high school, college and professional sports.

Finally, low cut blouses, T-shirts and clothes made from an American flag were never seen in the halls or classrooms of GHS. Shorts were only worn for gym class.

Gettysburg High School freshmen may have dressed differently than they do in 2015, but inside we were the same, anxious about our place in our new school and uncertain about the future.

Bruce at 14 dressed for church

DAD WESTERDAHL'S TOUR OF DISCOVERY

Back in the Forties, if you wanted to tour the site of the 1863 battle at Gettysburg, you could find a uniformed, licensed guide on the village square.

When Nancy and I were growing up in Gettysburg in the Forties, Dad Westerdahl often took our family visitors on a very unique Battlefield tour. Dad's trip covered the same sites as the licensed guides, but he added a few additional stops that weren't provided by an official guide.

For example, on a stone bridge over Plum Run on South Confederate Ave. there are three dinosaur footprints which were always part of Dad's tours. According to local practical jokers, the one pictured here was made by "anchisauripus sillimani, a lion sized meat eater that walked on two legs and roamed Pennsylvania 200 million years ago."

Another stop on Dad's tours, was a sulfur spring southwest of Gettysburg on or near the Water Works Rd. Sulphur water smells like rotten eggs, and it was a particular feature of York Sulphur Springs, the first summer resort in Adams County where George and Martha Washington came to bathe in their curative water.

Dad's "Tour of Discovery" often included a trip to Brooke Avenue on the Battlefield near Plum Run where a pair of Pileated Woodpeckers might be seen and heard in the forest there.

A tour in the spring of the year was sure to include visits west of Gettysburg to view huge fields of daffodils and another stop off Rt 15 south where a large-wooded area was covered with blue grape hyacinths.

Dad's unique and unforgettable tours often ended at dusk with a visit to a field off the Taneytown Road to check out a herd of deer that might be seen feeding on the new grass at the edge of the woods.

Licensed guides charged a fee for their tours. Dad's tours were free.

1945 FOOTBALL AND RETURNING VETERANS

The Gettysburg High School football team in 1945 ended their season in the middle of November with a 32-13 loss to Mechanicsburg. In seven straight losses, the team was outscored by a total of 155 points. In three consecutive seasons, the varsity football team won only one game. Students and all football fans in Gettysburg were hungry for a win.

On December 6, the Gettysburg Times reported absences in the Gettysburg Schools of more than 25 per cent. The wave of illnesses was the result of grippe and colds. Today, we call the "grippe" influenza.

With the end of World War II in 1945, our veterans were returning home in large numbers. On December 6, for example, ten countians were discharged from Indiantown Gap, the U.S. Army Post northeast of Harrisburg.

Sterrett "Duke" Dorsey, who left the Class of 1946 before graduation, did not come home to finish his degree. He died on December 3, 1945 of injuries sustained while serving in the Navy in the South Pacific. Twenty-five other graduates and former students of Gettysburg High School made the supreme sacrifice for their country in WWII.

Many of those who did return home after the war attended college on the GI Bill which paid for veterans' tuition and living expenses. The Gettysburg College basketball team boasted eight veterans playing during the 1945-46 season. Under coach Hen Bream, the team won seventy- five percent of their games and set a new gym scoring record against LaSalle winning 79-34.

NO TV BUT WE WERE ENTERTAINED

According to a website titled The History of Film, Television and Video, there were fewer than 7,000 working TV sets in the country in 1945. If there were any TVs in Gettysburg in 1945 when we were growing up there, neither Nancy or I knew about it.

The first TV we remember was in the window of Baker's Battery Service on Baltimore Street which was one of the first stores to sell TVs in Gettysburg. Because there were only nine stations on the air in 1945, and the closest was in Philadelphia, we doubt if there was a TV in Baker's window at that time.

In 1945 we found our entertainment in school activities, listening to music on the radio and records and going to the movies. It was not unusual to attend two movies a week, and each show included a cartoon and a newsreel as well as the feature film.

The Academy Award for the best film of 1945 was Lost Weekend, the story about an alcoholic writer on a four-day bender. Our favorite that year was *Anchors Aweigh*, a musical comedy starring Frank Sinatra and Gene Kelly. Both movies are available on YouTube.

Nancy's diaries reveal that she often listened to Your Hit Parade, a radio program that aired on Saturday nights. The popular program, sponsored by Lucky Strike cigarettes, played the most popular songs from the previous week. The two most popular songs in 1945, remained at number one for nine weeks. They were *Till the End of Time* by Perry Como and *Sentimental Journey* by Les Brown.

Despite the lack of TV in 1945, we were always entertained.

REMEMBERING PLEASANT AROMAS

Several students from Dr. Michael Birkner's Historical Methods course at Gettysburg College asked Nancy and me about our memories of specific streets in our hometown in 1945.

Responding to these requests has brought to mind places we haven't thought about since we left Gettysburg as a married couple sixty-two years ago.

One location is Ernie's Texas Lunch on Chambersburg Street between the Lutheran Church and Washington Street. With a menu that reminds guests of a diner from the Thirties, Ernie's features old favorites like chili cheese fries, onion rings and classic hot dogs including chili dogs and one with everything.

If you were blindfolded while walking on Chambersburg Street, you could find Ernie's Texas Lunch from the distinctive smell of onions, peppers and hot dogs cooking on the grill in the front window.

And if you crossed to the south side of the street, there was another business you could find with your nose before you saw it. A roasted peanut machine stood in front of George's shoe-shine parlor and shoe repair business, and for a couple of pennies, you could buy a small bag of roasted peanuts in their shells. The aroma of those hot roasted peanuts could be recognized up and down the block.

One more place we remember where the aroma was exhilarating was Henning's Bakery in the first block of York

89

Street. It was the wonderful scent of warm bread that stimulated the senses and made the place so memorable.

I hope our comments about places we remember in 1945 are helping the Gettysburg students with their history assignment. It certainly has been fun for us to recall the charm of those businesses mentioned above.

CHRISTMAS 1945

Christmas, 1945 was a very special time for millions of people in our Country. World War II was over, and those who had served in the armed forces here or overseas were welcomed home. For some, it had been three years or more since loved ones were together at Christmas.

Bing Crosby sang the most popular song in December 1945, and it expressed the sentiment of many when he sang, "Kiss me once and kiss me twice, and kiss me once again. It's been a long, long time."

Photo credit: Joyce Wiedrich
Gettysburg National Cemetery

I was in the Marine Corps from 1952 until 1955, and during that time, Nancy and I spent every Christmas apart. It was a painful experience, but my life was never threatened like those who served during the war.

Nancy's uncle who served as a chaplain in Italy and Germany, was discharged in August of 1945, and my Dad, who was a Seabee, was discharged in December of that year. It was a very happy Christmas for both families.

While millions of Americans celebrated the Holidays with loved ones when World War II ended, there were others mourning the loss of loved ones who never came home. Many would return, not as they left, but with serious injuries suffered in service of our country.

Nancy and I continue to observe Christmas in Gettysburg as participants in the National Wreath Project sponsored by the Sgt. Mac Organization. Each December we help decorate Christmas wreaths and place them on the graves in the National Cemetery. Members of the family we dreamed about when we fell in love in the Forties join us for this memorable experience.

COACH FORNEY AND BASKETBALL IN 1946

In January of 1946, George Forney returned to Gettysburg High School, after serving in the Navy during World War IL He immediately resumed his duties coaching the basketball team which finished the season winning seventeen games and losing only three.

In 1946, basketball was a very different game than fans watch today. First, we dressed differently. We wore black high-top sneakers, belted short shorts, sleeveless jerseys tucked into our shorts and black leather kneepads which no one wears today.

The free throw lane, or key, was only six feet wide in 1946. There was no three-point shooting, and there was no shot clock which meant a team could freeze the ball forever. The result was a game which emphasized defense more than teams do today.

When George Forney returned as coach in January of 1946, his team averaged 41 points a game and their opponents averaged only 29! In a conference game that season Gettysburg beat Waynesboro 45 to 6 which suggests that Waynesboro didn't score a goal in at least one period.

The freewheeling style of basketball we know as "run and gun" was never practiced while Nancy and I were at Gettysburg High School.

George Forney coached football, basketball and track at Gettysburg until his retirement in 1973.

He is a member of the Pennsylvania Sports Hall of Fame, and the current gymnasium at the high school bears his name. He died in 1993 at the age of 95.

Bruce wearing glasses

MORE ABOUT BASKETBALL IN THE FORTIES

We've heard from several friends who reminded us of other changes in the game since the Forties.

For example, I played basketball at Gettysburg High School for four years, and I don't remember anyone on our team slam-dunking the ball. I also don't recall anyone dunking the ball on the teams we played in the old South Penn Conference. It simply wasn't part of the game.

Today, when two or more opposing players have possession of the ball at the same time, the referee awards the ball to one team or the other on a rotating basis. Every held ball in the Forties resulted in a jump ball which occasionally resulted in a 5'6" guard jumping against a center a foot taller than him.

Today, a team is awarded free throws after their opponents accumulate a specific number of fouls. I don't recall such a rule when I played the game.

In the previous post about basketball seventy years ago, I mentioned there was no shot clock and more emphasis on defense. That resulted in much lower scores like a 20 - 13 win against Shippensburg in 1946.

But wait a minute! Apparently, defense in basketball is not dead. In November 2015, the Bibb County High School basketball team of Panther County, Alabama, defeated Brookwood High School 2-0. All the scoring happened in the first 15 seconds of the opening possession. The remaining 31-plus minutes were scoreless.

It is rumored the game was so dull that fans, players on the bench, a coach and one of the referees went to sleep. Me too had I been there.

Bruce posing for yearbook photo

NEWS FROM GETTYSBURG: JANUARY 1946

Nancy and I were lowly freshmen at Gettysburg High School and about to turn fourteen when the new year began in January of 1946. Both of us were honor roll students and involved in school activities like sports, student council and choir.

On the south end of town, the College announced the need for rooms to accommodate 150 veterans of World War II who were planning to begin the second semester at Gettysburg. Thanks to the GI bill which paid veterans to continue their schooling, nearly eight million veterans would participate in education and training programs throughout the country.

In January, Kathryn Oiler, librarian for the Adams County Free Library on Carlisle Street, announced the hours when the library would be open for the public.

Nancy and I remember the library across from High Street School and the library in the former Post Office on Baltimore Street but have no recollection of a library on Carlisle Street.

Also in January of 1946, members of the Chamber of Commerce were informed that Gettysburg was not chosen as the site for the United Nations peace capital. Gettysburg was one of forty areas that offered to host the intergovernmental organization established to promote international cooperation.

A front-page story in the *Gettysburg Star and Sentinel* on January 5, 1946, reported that someone broke into the local jail, but the culprit escaped.

TEEN CANTEEN: WINTER 1946

When Nancy and I were growing up in Gettysburg in the Forties, the Teen Canteen on Baltimore Street played a very significant role in our relationship. It was there on February 21, 1948 while slow dancing, I fell in love with the 17-year-old classmate who was to become my wife five long years later. But in 1946, we barely knew each other outside of the classes we shared together.

Nancy and I would come to know each other well in the fall of 1946 when we were elected officers in the sophomore class. The class picture in the 1947 yearbook is the first photo of us together.

The Teen Canteen in early 1946 was located in a former bank building on the east side of Baltimore Street just a few doors from Middle Street. It had become a popular place for high school kids to go, and in 1945, 108 people attended the Labor Day dance where an eight-piece orchestra entertained.

In an article in the *Maroon and White* in February of '46, high school students expressed their opinions about the Canteen. Freshman classmate Pat Shealer offered one of the most colorful comments saying, "It's a swell place to spend an evening. Hubba!" Senior Janice Cole said, "I like it for it gives the kids two things to do instead of one which is going to the movies."

The February *Maroon and White* also featured an article announcing the Canteen would soon be open two nights a week and not just Saturday.

DANCES AND PROMS

The Teen Canteen which was located in a former bank building on Baltimore Street. Unfortunately, the roof must have leaked and the water warped the wooden dance floor, but that didn't stop us from dancing to the popular music of the day.

We recently Googled the top twenty songs of 1945 and 1946, and we have danced to almost everyone, including ageless songs by Frank Sinatra, Perry Como and Harry James.

In addition to dancing at the Teen Canteen, the Student Council, Girls' Athletic Association and Girl Scouts often sponsored dances after home football and basketball games. Annual proms provided special occasions for dancing to the music of live bands.

Going to a prom in the Forties was nothing like it is today. Yes, the girls wore gowns, but the guys never wore tuxes. Also, we don't remember going to dinner and most certainly, we never rented limousines. And if people took pictures of us when we were dressed for a prom, we have none.

Our circle of friends didn't drink alcohol before, during or after a prom, and drugs of any kind were unheard of.

I asked Nancy to the Spring Prom in 1948, and we have been a couple from that time until today, 68 years later. I think I'll go ask her for a dance for old times' sake.

CONTEMPORARY WORDS UNKNOWN IN 1946

One of the most popular posts on Growing Up in Gettysburg referred to the slang words and phrases from the Forties that might not be understood by current high school students.

Now let's look at a few common words and phrases we currently use which would have drawn blank stares in the Forties. For example, if I asked a classmate in 1946 if he had seen my latest post on Facebook, he would have had no idea what I was talking about.

Here is a short list of words in our current vocabulary that would not be understood by people in the Forties: email, hi-tech, social media, morph, rock star, retro, global warming, climate change, video, meth and pixels.

These proper nouns were also unknown to us when we were growing up in Gettysburg in the Forties: iPhones, iCloud, iWatch, iBook, iPad, iMovie, iTunes, YouTube, Google, Hyundai, Amazon, Pay Pal, Corvette, Twitter, eBay and Buffalo wings.

In addition, there are many acronyms and abbreviations we all recognize today, but we never heard of in the Forties: NASA, TSA, AIDS, NSA, DEA, OSHA, NAFTA, ESPN, PBS, NOVA, AARP, IBM.

Finally, text messaging was an unknown method of communicating when we were in school, and the 1,424 abbreviations used in texting would be like Greek to anyone in the Forties. JSYK

BIKES AND BIKING

When Nancy and I were fifteen growing up in Gettysburg in the early Forties, we were too young to obtain a Driver's License or even a Learner's Permit. Our primary way to get around Gettysburg was to walk or ride our single-speed bikes. We never heard of or saw a 3-speed, 5-speed or any other speed bike.

Every business or home in the Borough of Gettysburg was and still is easily accessible by bike. For a leisurely ride, we headed to the Battlefield. Nancy would ride out Hancock Avenue toward the Pennsylvania Monument, and I would take East Confederate Avenue toward Spangler's Spring.

On a hot summer day, a popular destination was The Battlefield Swimming Pool south of Gettysburg on the Baltimore Pike. Informally known as Jack's Pool, it was not very big and only six-foot deep. It didn't take many teenagers before the pool was quite full.

Bikes in the forties had some distinct features you don't see today. The frame was heavier, we had fenders and our tires were much fatter than those on road bikes today. To customize our bikes, we added accessories like mud guards, a headlight and speedometer, a horn, rear view mirror and Texas handlebars, so called because they resembled the horns on a Texas Longhorn.

Nancy's favorite accessory was a wire basket mounted in front of her handlebars. The basket is where she put the groceries, but it was a lot more fun to put her small dog Daisy in the basket and take her for a ride.

One accessory that we never had and never saw was a helmet. We never saw a bicycle lock either. There was no need for a bicycle lock, one of the many advantages to growing up in a small town in the Forties.

Looking back at biking when we were growing up in Gettysburg is just one of many fond memories we have of our lives there in the Forties.

STUFF WE REMEMBER:

When our favorite radio shows were the *Aldrich Family*, *Fred Allen*, *Inner Sanctum*, *Jack Benny*, *Grand Ole Opry*, *Lux Radio Theater*, *Walter Winchell* and *Your Hit Parade*.

When we stopped for gas, someone cleaned our windshield, checked the oil, pumped the gas, air was free and we got green stamps.

Esso station in Newark, NJ

When we went to the movies, we always saw a cartoon.

When water balloons were the ultimate weapon.

When we made a telephone call, it was always placed through a switch-board operator, and many phones were on a party line.

When washing machines had ringers, we dumped the wash water on the garden, and we hung the wash on a line in the backyard.

When catching fireflies could happily occupy us for an entire evening.

When people sat on their front porch after dinner and greeted their neighbors passing by.

When we loved reading *The Saturday Evening Post* and *Life* each week.

When "Olly, Olly, Oxen Free" made perfect sense.

When everyone in your class had an autograph book and every classmate was invited to sign it.

When life's most embarrassing moment was being chosen last for a pick-up game.

AUTOGRAPHS AND HIGH SCHOOL YEARBOOKS

In the last chapter, we made a brief mention of autograph books which were popular in junior high schools back in the Forties. The idea was for each classmate to have his or her own book and to ask as many people as possible to sign it.

About twenty years ago, Nancy and I were looking through a box of memorabilia and we found the autograph books we started in eighth grade.

Everyone who signed Nancy's book, thought she was pretty sweet and said so with unoriginal verses like:

Roses are red violets are blue.
Sugar is sweet and so are you.

And:

Roses are red violets are blue.
No one I know is as nice as you.

The boys were a little more creative with their messages:

Roses are wilted and violets are dead.
The sugar is lumpy and so is your head!

We don't remember autograph books at Gettysburg High School. Perhaps that's because our yearbooks, signed by friends and popular students, were a substitute for autograph books.

We suppose that autograph books, like so many other customs from the Forties are no longer popular, but finding our books signed long ago helped us remember the friends of our youth, especially the friend who signed Nancy's book with this memorable verse:

"When memory with her golden key unlocks the past, remember me."

We hope this book is a "golden key" that helps readers unlock the past in our hometown.

NEW CARS ARE BACK

An article in the February 28, 2016 issue of *Automotive News* revealed that within two months of the December 7, 1941 bombing of Pearl Harbor, the last civilian car came off the assembly line, and auto manufacturers began making tanks, halftracks and numerous other vehicles for the war effort.

When Nancy and I were growing up in Gettysburg in 1945, World War II was coming to an end, and in July of that year, wartime restrictions on automotive production ended.

Once again, factories throughout the country began concentrating on making cars for the general public.

In March of 1946, one of the first cars to arrive in Gettysburg was the new DeSoto Deluxe with fluid drive. It was on display at Phiel's Garage on York Street, and it was the first new model since 1942.

An article in the *Star & Sentinel* in March of 1946 reported that more than 400 people visited the Glenn C. Bream car dealer on Chambersburg Street in Gettysburg to see the new Plymouth and the new Chrysler.

The earliest mention of a new Ford we discovered in the Gettysburg area was a report of an accident in May involving a 1946 model.

The end of the war meant new cars and the end of gas rationing. As a result, the local Chamber of Commerce reported that inquiries more than tripled in the first two months of 1946 compared to the same period in 1945. The tourists would soon return to Gettysburg!

A 1946 Plymouth

DISCOVERING GETTYSBURG

In 1953, Nancy and I left our hometown of Gettysburg where we grew up in the Forties, but we return several times each year to see old friends and to participate in the National Wreath Project sponsored by the Sgt. Mac Memorial Foundation.

When we were growing up in Gettysburg, one of our favorite pastimes was to hike areas of the Battlefield few tourists ever see.

Photo courtesy of the Library of Congress
Devil's Den - One of many places to explore

When we were young, we explored the woods south of Williams Avenue below Culp's Hill where we discovered a small quarry. We have also wandered along Rock Creek from Third Bridge on East Confederate Avenue to the Baltimore Pike.

For Nancy and me, the Gettysburg National Park was, and continues to be a place of discovery. Over many years, we have discovered a wide variety of birds and flowers, trails, meadows and memorials to individuals and units who fought there.

Millions of people learn important lessons of history when they visit Gettysburg each year. When Nancy and I were growing up there in the Forties, we had many experiences, but our greatest discovery was in 1948 when we realized we were in love.

MORE SLANG FROM THE FORTIES

In one of our most popular posts on this blog, Nancy and I wrote about the slang words people used when we were growing up in Gettysburg in the Forties. Here are a few more words and phrases from that decade that we don't hear any longer.

One slang word I will never forget, because I heard it often is knucklehead. According to the *Urban Dictionary*, a knucklehead was a "person of questionable intelligence whose brain was the size of his knuckle."

I was familiar with the word because it was the favorite expression of the Gettysburg High School football coach when someone, like me, failed an assignment. Strangely, I don't remember what we were called when we did something right and well. I don't think he had a word for that.

Back in the Forties, people were permitted on the Battlefield after dark, and Nancy and I remember a night when we parked on Oak Ridge to discuss the news of the day. When we were ready to leave, I turned the key to start the car, and it broke off in my hand. In that awkward situation, I might have said, "Now this is a fine kettle of fish," meaning, "We have a problem!" No one talks about fish in a kettle in situations like that any longer.

People don't talk about jalopies anymore either. Back in the Forties, an old car in poor condition was referred to as a jalopy, and there were a lot more on the road than we see today.

GETTYSBURG PREPARES FOR THE SUMMER OF '46

In the spring of 1946, officials connected to the tourist trade in Gettysburg where Nancy and I grew up in the Forties, expected the busiest tourist season since before World War II.

In April of that year, Superintendent of the Gettysburg National Park, J. Walter Coleman, reported that travel over the battlefield in 1946 was expected to be the same or above pre-war averages.

In preparation for the thousands of tourists, additional staff was added to repair fences and signs and restore roads to pre-war condition.

The biggest event in Gettysburg in the spring of 1946 occurred on May 27 when General Dwight D. "Ike" Eisenhower, Chief of Staff of the United States Army and the former supreme commander of the Allied Forces in Europe, spoke at the Gettysburg College Commencement.

One special feature of that event was the dedication of a plaque honoring the 60 men from Gettysburg College who gave their lives during World War II.

In the spring of 1946, Nancy played intra-class field hockey and I lettered in varsity track. That year, the track team won all the meets and the Conference Championship by an average of 30 points. Back in the Forties, there were no lacrosse, baseball or softball teams.

GETTYSBURG HIGH SCHOOL: SPRING OF 1946

In the spring of 1946 when Nancy and I were freshmen at Gettysburg High School, track and field was the only varsity sport offered to students, and girls could not participate. Gettysburg teams dominated in track and field in the South Penn Conference throughout the Forties.

I tried to compare current track and field records at Gettysburg High School with times and distances records from the Forties, but so much has changed, it is practically impossible. For example, all track records are now in meters instead of yards which were used when we were in school.

High school track teams currently compete in the weights as we did in the Forties, but the discus and javelin are now weighed in kilograms not pounds. The shot put still weighs 12 pounds as it did in the Forties, and the current Gettysburg record of 50' 5.5" is more than 5' further than the record for that event was in the Forties.

The introduction of the Fosbury Flop in the high jump in 1965 and the flexible pole in vaulting in the early Fifties revolutionized those events, and today, high school athletes, both male and female, jump and vault much higher than we did in the Forties.

It would be many years before the girls competed against other schools in Conference play in any sport, but on May 18, 1946 the Gettysburg High Girls' Athletic Association invited their sister GAA Club from Hanover for a Play Day involving games in basketball, kickball and volleyball.

MEMORIAL DAY PARADE 1946

When Nancy and I were growing up in Gettysburg in the Forties, we always looked forward to the Memorial Day Parade in May. The event in 1946 was special, because it was the first peace-time observance of Memorial Day since 1941.

Following police escorts and the parade marshals, the Gettysburg High School Band led 1,000 school children dressed in white and carrying flowers which were later strewn on the graves in the National Cemetery. It's a tradition that continues to this day.

Veterans from World War I and World War II marched with bands, drum and bugle corps, community organizations, and members of the Veterans of Foreign Wars and American Legion. A unit of the Pennsylvania National Guard with motorized equipment was followed by the speaker John Bricker, the former Governor of Ohio, and honored guests.

The 1946 Memorial Day Parade was reported in the press as one of the biggest in Gettysburg's history. Nancy's home in the Forties was on Baltimore Street, the perfect place to watch a Memorial Day Parade, and every year friends and family would gather in front of her house in lawn chairs to enjoy the spectacle. A picnic for family and guests always followed the parade.

May was also time for the annual spring concert at Gettysburg High School. In 1946, the concert included a number by the freshman chorus which was accompanied by Nancy Ogden. And "No," Nancy Ogden and Bruce Westerdahl were not a couple yet, and we probably weren't even dancing together then. That would happen in the fall of 1947.

SUMMER OF 1946

Nancy and I were not yet sixteen when we were growing up in Gettysburg in the summer of 1946, so we were not eligible for a work permit. Nancy helped her mother with summer chores like canning and freezing fruits and vegetables. She also helped her father in the garden where they grew tomatoes and string beans.

Even though I didn't have a work permit, I was employed as a member of the ground crew at Camp Nawakwa, a Lutheran camp twenty minutes northwest of Gettysburg. I worked on construction projects, mowed and dug ditches for a new waterline.

The altar at Fischer Chapel

Summers in Gettysburg in 1946 could be unbearably hot and humid, so Nancy and I swam often. She cooled off in the Battlefield Swimming Pool south of Gettysburg, and I swam in the pool at camp which was always freezing. On weekends, we often picnicked with family at any one of numerous parks in Adams County.

TV was not yet popular in 1946, so we found our entertainment listening to the radio or going to one of the two Warner Brothers Theaters in Gettysburg. There was a Teen Canteen in town in 1946, and we remember that it was located in the first block of Baltimore Street in an abandoned bank building.

In August, the *Gettysburg Times* reported that Burgess C. A. Heiges instructed borough police to begin enforcing the town's 1917 curfew which provides that during Standard Time all youngsters under 18 years of age must be off the streets of town by 9:00. During Daylight Savings Time the curfew limit would be 10:00 p.m.

Nancy and I remember no curfews so we assume this law was rescinded sometime later that year.

A MOST IMPORTANT PERSON

Nancy and I have said very little about the people who were a part of our lives, i.e., parents, siblings, teachers and friends, so let us begin to correct that omission by describing the most important people in our lives when we were fifteen, our parents.

In the Forties, Nancy lived with her mother, dad and older brother, Bill, at the base of Baltimore Street hill in a white two story, four-bedroom house that may have existed during the Battle of Gettysburg. Often, Nancy's home was also opened to loved ones who were no longer able to live alone.

Nancy's mother (Grace Hartman) was a teacher who graduated from Gettysburg Academy to prepare for Shippensburg State Teachers College where she was certified after just two years. Her first teaching assignment was in a one-room schoolhouse in East Berlin.

She and Nancy's father were married in 1924, and after the service, they moved directly to a home on Liberty Street which was already paid for. Her Dad was a banker, and in 1924, he believed you didn't buy anything until you had the money to pay for it.

Grace Hartman Ogden was beloved by family and friends. She was known for her fried oysters, pot pie with homemade noodles, crab cakes and hog-maw. She had a deep committed faith in her God, and she was faithful to her family who she

117

served unselfishly throughout her life. She lived a life that is celebrated and admired by her family and friends.

Grace Hartman Ogden

ANOTHER IMPORTANT PERSON

In the last chapter, we described a most important person in Nancy's life while she was growing up in Gettysburg, her mother, Grace Hartman Ogden.

Here, we choose to comment on an important person in my life, my mother, Elizabeth Houck Westerdahl.

Mother was only three when she saw her own mother, Elsie Pearl Clopper, buried in York, Pennsylvania. Her mother was descended from Cornelius Janzen Clopper who arrived in New Amsterdam (Manhattan) in 1630.

Elizabeth loved to cook for large family dinners and her expertise in the kitchen was admired and enjoyed by everyone. One of the secrets of her culinary skills was a generous amount of butter and cream in many of her dishes, but despite those risks to good health in her own diet, mother lived to be 101 aided by good genes by those who preceded her.

From her home on Lincoln Avenue in Gettysburg, mother walked to work at the Bookmart on Chambersburg Street every day for many years. What better place to be employed than a bookstore since reading was her life-long hobby and passion?

Throughout her life, Elizabeth was fastidious about her personal appearance and anxious about the image projected by her family. When in public, she was well groomed and well dressed, and she expected as much from her family.

119

Mother Westerdahl had a stroke in January of 2010. For the next five days, she smiled and laughed with those who loved her most, then she died quietly in her sleep, content that she had lived a long and satisfying life.

Elizabeth Houck Westerdahl

A TRAGIC LOSS

Nancy and I have many memories of growing up in Gettysburg, but not all our reminiscences are happy and treasured. We were reminded of that when we recently turned the pages of our 1946 Gettysburg High School yearbook in which the events of our freshman year are recorded.

1946 yearbook dedicated to General Eisenhower

The yearbook was dedicated to General Dwight David Eisenhower who guided our military through the European Theater of War in World War II. The reference to the war was a reminder that world-wide 60 million people were casualties of that conflict. One page of the 1946 yearbook listed the names of 26 alumni of Gettysburg High School who lost their lives in World War II.

Turning the pages of the yearbook to a photograph of our freshman class along with a list of names, we recognized one name that reminded us of a tragic event that occurred as our class was about to begin our sophomore year.

On Monday, August 26, 1946, our classmate Sydney Poppay was thrown from a pick-up truck as he returned to Gettysburg after picking peaches at one of the local fruit farms. Brought to the Warner hospital, our friend and classmate died of a fractured skull and other injuries the next morning.

Sydney was a good student who was involved in his church, his scout troop and in school activities. Had he lived, he would have continued to be a valuable and contributing member of our class and our school. Three years later, our senior yearbook acknowledged our loss with these words:

"We remember with love and respect Sydney Poppay, a schoolmate of ours for a number of years, who was with us but one year during our high school days... His spirit still abides in the circles that his presence once graced."

PREPARING FOR A NEW FOOTBALL SEASON

When Nancy and I were preparing for our sophomore year at Gettysburg High School in 1946, everyone was looking forward to the coming football season. After winning only one game during the two previous seasons, the coaches, the team and the fans appreciated new opportunities for a winning team.

Pre-season drills began on August 19 at a Masonic Camp south of Gettysburg under new head coach, George Forney who returned the previous February to teach and coach after serving two years in the Navy during World War II.

At camp, the team was introduced to Coach Forney's very unconventional version of the single wing formation. The single wing featured four linemen and three backs on one side of the center and was considered a brute force running formation described by some as "three yards and a cloud of dust." Passing was rare in the Forties, and several coaches are credited with saying, "Three things can happen when you throw a pass and two of them are bad."

The 1946 football season was my first opportunity to play varsity football, and I hoped that my enthusiasm and determination would allow me to earn a place on the starting team. Incidentally, in 1946 team members played both offense and defense. The popular two platoon system we recognize in high school, college and professional football was used by very few teams at that time.

It would not be long before Gettysburg fans would learn if the 1946 high school team would produce some overdue wins. Our first game was at Delone Catholic High School on September 13.

1946-47 SCHOOL YEAR BEGINS

In September of 1946, Nancy and I were beginning our sophomore year at Gettysburg High School in the historic town where we grew up. The big news that fall was that tourist travel to Gettysburg returned to near normal since prior to World War II.

Family on the Pennsylvania Monument

The National Park Service estimated that 508,641 visitors toured the Battlefield during the 1946 tourist season. Today, Gettysburg attracts well over a million visitors during the same period each year. Heavy traffic and large crowds are two major changes we notice when Nancy and I visit our hometown.

Early in the school year in 1946, students at Gettysburg High School were asked to vote for class officers. Strangely, two of the students elected by the sophomores would ultimately spend a lifetime together. Nancy was elected secretary of the class, and I was elected president.

Two years later, Nancy and I would fall in love, and seven years later we were married. In 2016, Nancy and I celebrated our sixty-third wedding anniversary.

In our last post we promised to report the result of the first football game in '46. On September 13, we lost to a seasoned Delone team 13-6. At times, it looked like our team would end the long drought that resulted in a single win the two previous seasons. A fumble in the final period on our own 31, led to the Delone win.

"Don't be discouraged," Coach Forney told us later. "We will win games this year!"

NOVELTY SONGS FROM THE FORTIES

When Nancy and I were sophomores at Gettysburg High School in 1946, the music we enjoyed on the radio or our record players included songs with beautiful and unforgettable lyrics like:

"Hey! Ba-Ba-Re-Bop (Hey! Ba-Ba-Re-Bop),
Hey! Ba-Ba-Re-Bop (Hey! Ba-Ba-Re-Bop),
Hey! Ba-Ba-Re-Bop (Hey! Ba-Ba-Re-Bop)
Hey! Hey! Ba-Ba-Re-Bop (Hey! Ba-Ba-Re-Bop)
Hey! Ba-Ba-Re-Bop (Hey! Ba-Ba-Re-Bop),
Yeah, my baby knows."

And who can forget the memorable and catchy lyrics to Mairzy Doats?

"Mairzy doats and dozy doats,
And liddle lamzy divey
A kiddley divey too, wooden shoe."

Some people called them novelty songs. Others referred to them as nonsense songs. In any case, the peculiar thing is that to this day Nancy and I are cursed to remember all the words to these and numerous other stupid songs but have trouble remembering what we ate for lunch two days ago.

Some years ago, I did a program of nonsense songs for a group of senior citizens, and most of them enthusiastically sang the lyrics like they had just heard them recently.

We suspect that such music was not meant for dancing but primarily for our listening pleasure either on the radio or on a 78rpm record we could play over and over until the words were imbedded in our memories.

Let's end our brief description of novelty tunes with the lyrics for Chi Baba Chi Baba which was recorded by Perry Como in 1947 and went to number one on the Billboard chart:

"Chi-baba, chi-baba, chi-wawa,
An' chi-lawa kook-a la goombah,
Chi-baba, chi-baba, chi-wawa,
My bambino go to sleep."

FORTIES TECHNOLOGY

Recently, a friend grumbled about technology and how much time her young children spend entertaining themselves on their smartphones. Her complaint prompted Nancy and me to recall the technology available to us when we were growing up in Gettysburg in the Forties.

For example, we had one telephone in each home, and neither was push button or dial up. We simply picked up the receiver from the cradle and an operator asked, "Number please." If I were calling Nancy, I would say,"29W." We couldn't take, send or receive a picture with the phone, we couldn't ask Siri questions, and we couldn't walk around with the phone, because it was connected to the wall by a wire.

Another miracle of technology in the Forties was the jukebox. One of our favorite places to dance was Woodlawn where they had a colorful and sophisticated Wurlitzer jukebox that played 78 rpm records. We can still remember dancing to all the popular music of the day by Frank, Bing, Dinah, Perry or Tex Beneke and the Glenn Miller Orchestra.

Two other entertainment technologies we enjoyed were the movies and the radio. As I write today, my radio is playing music of the Forties, and I am reminded that radio still remains a favorite after all these years.

Readers will recall that we promised to report on Gettysburg High School football in 1946. After we lost the first game to Delone 13-6, Coach Forney told us we would win games that season. We didn't have to wait long, because we beat York Catholic in the next game 19-0. The victory broke a 12-game losing streak that extended back to 1944. Big Joe Hess was responsible for all the points. The win was particularly sweet for a team that was victory starved for three seasons.

RADIO JINGLES IN THE FORTIES

In our last post about growing up in Gettysburg in the Forties, Nancy and I mentioned that radio was one of our most popular forms of entertainment when we were teenagers. Singing commercials, or jingles as we called them, were a significant part of radio at that time.

The singing commercial can be traced back to before World War II, and our earliest recollection of jingles coincides with that fact. The very first singing commercial on the radio we remember was sponsored by Pepsi-Cola about 1939. Here are the lyrics to that popular jingle:

"Pepsi-Cola hits the spot, twelve full ounces that's a lot.
Twice as much for a nickel too.
Pepsi-Cola is the drink for you."

The message in the jingle was almost true. The familiar, contoured Coke bottle was 6.5 ounces, but the slight discrepancy didn't hinder new Pepsi drinkers who quickly increased the latter's share of the market as a result of the jingle. It took Coke sixteen years to respond to Pepsi's challenge before introducing a larger size bottle.

Many of the early radio ads were based on popular folk songs, such as the Camel cigarette jingle which was sung to the tune of Eating Goober Peas.

"Rich, rich, mild, mild Camel cigarettes,
Rich, rich, rich with flavor, Camel cigarettes."

Now let us report on the 1946 season of the Gettysburg High School football team whose victory over York Catholic broke a twelve-game losing streak that began two years earlier.

Unfortunately, the team lost to Carlisle in the game that followed, but in our next post we will have news about a surprising and stunning victory over a traditional rival.

THE THRILL OF VICTORY

I was a lowly sophomore in October of 1946 playing in my fourth Gettysburg High School varsity football game, and the team was scheduled to meet Hanover on their field.

Hanover, a team we had not beaten in ten years, was undefeated that season, and they were clearly favored.

Hanover v. Gettysburg

Given the odds against us, over 4,000 fans were undoubtedly surprised when the fourth quarter began and neither team had scored. Then, with six minutes left, our fullback big Joe Hess plowed through right guard for the first score of the game.

Back in the Forties football coaches were not enthusiastic about passing, and that was certainly true in our game with Hanover that night when we only passed the ball four times, three for completions. Fortunately, I was on the receiving end for at least one pass, and it was good for the extra point, and we took the lead 7-0.

The drama was not over. With two minutes to play, Hanover also scored a touchdown, but missed the place kick for the extra point.
Underrated Gettysburg High School won the game 7-6.

Imagine our surprise when the team bus returned to Gettysburg, and we were greeted by hundreds of fans including Nancy. Escorted by those enthusiastic fans and the high school band, the team paraded from our school to Baltimore Street and then up to the square where the celebration continued.

I played high school and college football for seven years and was part of many good teams, but no win was as sweet as the victory over Hanover that chilly October night in 1946 when I was just fifteen.

THE ADAMS COUNTY LIBRARY

In an earlier chapter, Nancy and I wrote about the Adams County Library which opened in January of 1945 when we were freshmen at Gettysburg High School.

Many years ago, Barb Seiferd, a member of the Class of '49, gave us copies of our school newspaper, the Maroon and White, published when we were students. Recently, I found an article in the November 20, 1946 issue reporting that the Library's collection now totaled 8,000 books.

That article prompted us to recall the changes we observed in the Library as it moved from Carlisle Street to the former jail building on High Street to the current location on Baltimore Street, formerly the Gettysburg Post Office.

One of the most dramatic changes in the Library is the increase in the number of volumes now available to the public. To determine that total, I called the Library and was informed by the staff that there are now 172,156 books in the collection.

The article from the 1946 *Maroon and White* also reported that 36,000 books were borrowed the previous year, and over 60 percent were borrowed from the Bookmobile. The Bookmobile continues to be a major asset today as it visits over fifty locations throughout Adams County. What a joy that must be for the children throughout the County when they see the Bookmobile arrive at their school.

134

I have no proof, but I feel certain Nancy and I were among the original members of the Library which has served the people of Adams County so well since we were freshmen at Gettysburg High School.

1946 FOOTBALL SEASON AND BIG JOHN HUZVAR

When Nancy and I were sophomores at Gettysburg High School in the fall of 1946, our varsity football team won three games and lost six. At least, we were no longer the Conference doormat.

What I remember best about playing football in 1946 is defeating Hanover for the first time in ten years, but I also remember the worst defeat of any team I ever played for in high school or college.

That was the night I met Big John Huzvar the fullback for Hershey High School.

John Huzvar was 6 feet 4 inches tall and he weighed 247 pounds when he played fullback for North Carolina State, the Philadelphia Eagles and the Baltimore Colts. As a senior at Hershey High School, he probably weighed less, but when he came roaring around my end on a sweep, it looked to me like Huzvar was already a pro and was loaned to Hershey for the night.

I was 5 ft 10 in, weighed 157 pounds and was almost two years younger. I distinctly remember John loping toward me on legs that must have carried him ten or twelve feet with every long stride. It took Big John just under two long threatening steps to get to me bravely guarding the Gettysburg left flank.

I used to think John Huzvar ran over me and left his cleat marks in my back, but I have reconsidered my actions that night, and now I'm almost certain I made a feeble attempt to tackle Big John but bounced off of him several feet as he rumbled up the sideline for a long gain.

That night, Big John Huzvar scored fourteen points. That night, Big John Huzvar would have scored more if he were given the ball a few more times. That night Big John Huzvar was a man competing against boys. The final score was 42 - 0. It was the worst "whoopin'" I ever experienced.

For more information about the truck I tried to tackle that crisp November night in 1946, Google "John Huzvar."

MEMORIES OF THE GETTYSBURG NATIONAL CEMETERY

Each year on November 19, residents and honored guests gather in the Gettysburg National Cemetery to remember the occasion when President Lincoln delivered his famous Gettysburg Address on the same date in 1863. When Nancy and I were sophomores at Gettysburg High School in 1946, students were dismissed early to attend the 83rd anniversary program.

More than a thousand persons grouped around the Soldiers National Monument which the local print media reported "marks the spot where Lincoln spoke." That same article indicated that the main speaker, Congressman Jennings Randolph, "stood where Lincoln stood."

The fact is that President Lincoln did not deliver his famous Gettysburg Address in the National Cemetery because there were open graves and fresh reburials everywhere. The dedication ceremony in 1863 occurred in the adjacent Evergreen Cemetery which, incidentally, is where Nancy's parents and many of her relatives are buried.

When we were growing up in Gettysburg, Nancy's home was at the bottom of the Baltimore Street hill before it rises again to Cemetery Hill. If she had lived there in 1863, she could have waved to President Lincoln going to the dedication ceremony and returning to the diamond as the center of Gettysburg was known then.

138

When Nancy and I were dating, we often walked through the beautifully landscaped Gettysburg National Cemetery. We still visit the hallowed ground each December to participate in the Christmas Wreath Program sponsored by the Sgt Mac Foundation.

Each year, hundreds of volunteers prepare Christmas wreaths which are placed on the headstones of graves in the Gettysburg and Quantico National Cemeteries. The project was initiated by the parents of Marine Corps Sergeant and Gettysburg native Eric McColley, who was killed in the line of duty in 2006.

Nancy and daughter Tammy

THANKSGIVING 1946

From mid-1945 to mid-1947, approximately 90 percent of the 12 million servicemen and women who participated in World War II for the United States were discharged.

Thanksgiving in 1946 was a time for many Americans to be truly grateful. World War II was over and millions of servicemen and women had returned home to their families and loved ones.

Yet there were homes where Thanksgiving in 1946 would be quiet and reflective, because a loved one who was killed in the war was not present. Over 400,000 Americans gave their lives for their country during the war.

In Gettysburg where Nancy and I grew up in the Forties Dr. Henry Hansen, president of Gettysburg College, told Rotarians, "The whole world is in a position where it ought to sit down and be thankful for the things it does have and the hopes it has for the future."

Incidentally, a full course Thanksgiving turkey dinner including soup, salad and dessert at Mitchell's Restaurant on the square in 1946 cost $1.25.

At Gettysburg High School in early December, 700 fans celebrated the beginning of basketball season with a win over St. Francis Prep School 29-25. In the first period of the game, neither team was able to locate the basket. As a result, the score at the end of the first period was 4-2. At half time, Gettysburg was winning 16-6. Obviously, there was no shot clock in 1946.

OBSELETE EXPRESSIONS

When Nancy and I were growing up in Gettysburg in the Forties, our parents and grandparents used expressions which are rarely heard today.

For example, when I was an annoying juvenile, I dropped a water balloon on my kid brother from a second story window. When my Mother saw it, she shouted a stern, "What the Sam Hill are you doing?" Many years later I learned the phrase "What the Sam Hill?," can be traced back to the 1830s and is simply a sanitized version of "What the hell?"

Back in the Forties, when Nancy brought home a report card with straight A's, her Mother might say, "Now that's the cat's meow." meaning she considered her report to be outstanding. I don't remember what my parents said when they saw my report card.

We no longer hear the phrase, "Holy Toledo!" used to express astonishment. I have been to Toledo, Ohio, and it's not holy by any standard, but in Toledo, Spain, there are 172 cathedrals, and that's a remarkable bit of trivia. Perhaps that's where that phrase originated.

Growing up in the Forties, we occasionally heard the phrase, "Faster than Jack Robinson." Surprisingly, that phrase was around long before Jackie Robinson played baseball for the Brooklyn Dodgers. According to Wikipedia, Jack Robinson was an English gentleman in the 19th century who changed his mind so often you had to be quick to catch him in a decision.

Obsolete words and phrases are part of our heritage, and even if we haven't heard one in a "month of Sundays," when we do, it brings back fond memories of growing up with our "kinfolk." We haven't heard that word recently either.

CHRISTMAS SEASON 1946

The 1946 Christmas Season in Gettysburg where Nancy and I grew up was packed with a variety of memorable activities for two busy and enthusiastic high school sophomores.

On Sunday evening, December 15, we attended a Christmas Concert by the Gettysburg College Choir at the Majestic Theater. The following Sunday, we were part of the crowd that attended the Christmas Concert at the Majestic Theater performed by The Blue and Gray Band.

The month of December was filled with numerous opportunities for dancing sponsored by the Student Council, the Elks Club, the Gettysburg High School Alumni, and the Teen Canteen.

Nancy was an avid and adept dancer, and by December 1946 I was no longer shy about dancing with girls, so we are certain we attended most, if not all, those events. Unfortunately, I was taught an unorthodox style of slow dancing, and that led to some awkward stumbling with my partners.

Obviously, after seventy years, there is much we have forgotten, but we still have vivid memories of two events that occurred during the Christmas Season in 1946 and are still popular today.

The Christmas Song, subtitled *Chestnuts Roasting on the Open Fire*, was released by Capital records in December of 1946. The song, featuring Nat King Cole, has an ageless charm, and I still get choked up when I hear it.

144

The ultimate holiday classic movie, *It's A Wonderful Life* starring Jimmy Stewart, made its premier in December of 1946, and ultimately, became one of the most popular movies of the 20th Century.

The Christmas Song and *It's a Wonderful Life* continue to remind us of 1946 when we were teenagers growing up in Gettysburg.

WINTER 1947

The resources available to Nancy and me as we write about growing up in Gettysburg in the Forties include her diaries from 1947, 1948 and 1949. She was very faithful to record her activities every day, and we will refer to her journals often as we continue to post entries on our blog.

For example, in early January of '46, Nancy wrote that it snowed 3-4 inches. When we read that, we tried to recall snow days when school was closed because of bad weather. We couldn't. A Google search supported our recollection.

A headline in the February 21, 1947 issue of the *Gettysburg Times* reported that 15-18 inches of snow fell in Adams County the previous day. As a result, schools in six county communities closed in the afternoon, but Gettysburg Schools were open all day with about 50 percent in attendance.

Nancy and I never realized we were such a hearty people.

Nancy's January 1947 diary reveals she was a dedicated player and fan of basketball. She participated in basketball for a sophomore club team, went to all varsity and JV home games and most away games, attended Gettysburg College home games and even attended a few junior high games.

One varsity game Nancy didn't see occurred at Hershey on January 10. Here's how it was reported in the *Gettysburg Times*:

"A one-handed field goal by Bruce Westerdahl in the last five seconds of play gave the Gettysburg High Maroons a thrilling 36-34 victory over Hershey in a South Penn league."

In the eight years I played high school and college basketball, I don't recall many games, but that shot and that win are permanently fixed in my mind.

OUR HISTORIC CHURCH

When Nancy and I were growing up in Gettysburg, we were members of the historic Evangelical and Reformed church on South Stratton Street. We went to Sunday School, attended worship services and sang in the youth choir.

Nancy the bride in Tom Thumb Wedding

On July 1, 1863, the first day of the Battle of Gettysburg, Union troops fighting north of the town were overwhelmed by Confederates under Jubal Early. As the defeated units retreated through Gettysburg, wounded men were brought to the church which served as a hospital.

148

Sergeant Reuben Ruch wrote that at least ten operating tables were set up in a lower room where holes were drilled in the wooden floor to let the blood drain.

There is also evidence that the bell tower of the church was used by Confederate sharpshooters, probably men from the Louisiana Tigers who occupied that area of Gettysburg until July 4.

On Tuesday, May 21, 1936, when she was five, Nancy was bride in a Tom Thumb wedding in the church involving more than forty children. The wedding was so well attended, an overflow crowd required a second performance the following day.

Seventeen years later, on May 30, 1953, Nancy and I were married in our church giving her the unusual distinction of being married three times in the same church to two different grooms.

A VALENTINE PARTY IN 1947

Nancy's 1947 diary reveals that on February 14, she attended a Valentine Party where ten boys and girls were present. Her diary also notes that they danced, ate and played Coffee Pot. Then they enjoyed playing the kissing game, Post Office.

We recently mentioned the party and the games at a family gathering and were greeted with blank stares. We were particularly surprised that no one heard of Post Office. It is time to enlighten our grandchildren and great-grandchildren about the games we played when we were growing up in Gettysburg in the Forties.

In Coffee Pot, one player is separated from the others who are asked to come up with a noun, for example, house, dog, tree, shoe. The separated player returns to the group and by asking a series of questions using "coffee pot" in place of the noun, the player has to guess the word.

For example, "Can you eat a coffee pot?" "Is a coffee pot alive?" The other players answer "yes" or "no." If the guessing player correctly identifies the word, the player who last answered the question is the next guesser.

At the Valentine Party in 1947, it was time to get down to more serious interaction in an exciting game of Post Office. To play, a boy is chosen to be the postman, and that person leaves the room. Then a girl is chosen to "check her mail." She knocks on the Post Office door, and when she is admitted, they kiss. Nancy remembers checking her mail often when one particular boy was the Postmaster.

We wonder how many boys and girls experienced their first kiss playing Post Office?

WE WERE A HEARTY BUNCH

In her diary for Thursday, February 20, 1947, Nancy wrote, "It snowed all day today. It's real deep and it's drifting." The following day, she wrote, "The snow is from 15-18 inches deep. Only 50% of the kids got to school today, but we had classes anyway!"

On Friday, the Gettysburg Times reported that "schools throughout the County were closed in the afternoon as a result of the snowstorm." Yet Gettysburg High School remained opened with 50% of the students attending, and Lincoln School for sixth, seventh and eighth grades was open with 85% of the students in attendance.

When Nancy and I were growing up in Gettysburg in the Forties, "Townies" walked to school or hitched a ride with someone who drove. Those who walked to school on Friday, February 21, battled huge drifts and wind described by the Times as "twisting and biting." Obviously, we were a vigorous and hearty bunch back in the Forties.

On Friday, the *Times* also reported that "All County schools announced that basketball games scheduled for tonight have been postponed until later dates." According to Nancy's diary, the *Times* was wrong. The Gettysburg basketball team played Waynesboro and beat them 45-36. It was our tenth win in 19 games.

Following the game, there was a dance which Nancy attended "for a little while" with friends. By 1949, the Friday night dances after basketball games would be a normal routine for Nancy and me as a couple.

An article on the sports page of the Times on February 22 reported that Stan Musial, the National Leagues' batting champion and most valuable player has not yet signed a contract because the St. Louis Cardinals refused to pay him the $30,000 he demanded.

Bryce Harper, the National League MVP in 2015, is playing for the Washington Nationals with a two-year contract which will pay him $3,750,000 this year.

SPRING SPORTS, DATES AND DANCES

The spring of 1947 was a time for spring sports, dating and dancing for Nancy and me growing up in Gettysburg as sophomores in high school.

The 1947 baseball season was a first for Gettysburg High School since 1936, and it began with a 10-6 convincing win over Shippensburg on the home field. Our classmate, Ronnie Kump who went on to play professional baseball, went 2-4 with a home run in the fourth inning.

The Gettysburg track team began the season with a win over nine Class A schools in the Shippensburg State Teachers College Invitational. Throughout the season, I participated in the 110-yard low hurdles with success and the high jump and broad jump with a few victories.

In the spring of 1947, Nancy participated in a softball program sponsored by the Girls Athletic Association and a club team sponsored by a Youth Group.

Nancy's diary for 1947 reveals that In March of that year, she asked a boy to the Leap Week Dance and then the Sadie Hawkins Day Dance the following Saturday. Nothing shy about this sophomore girl. In May, the same boy invited Nancy to be his date at the Spring Prom.

Incidentally, this classmate just happened to be the boy she played Post Office with back in February at a Valentine's Party.

Undoubtedly, Nancy danced to songs by the most popular singers in the Spring of 1947 who were Vaughn Monroe, Dick Haymes, Peggy Lee, Frank Sinatra, Bing Crosby and Nancy's favorite, Perry Como. We still hear their music on several channels on Sirius Radio.

MORE ABOUT THE SPRING OF 1947

Students who played varsity sports at Gettysburg High School in the spring of 1947 were pleased with the results. The track team went undefeated while setting several new school records, and in their first season since 1936, the varsity baseball team won five games and lost three.

The biggest event in national sports in the spring of 1947 was the news that Jackie Robinson joined the Brooklyn Dodgers to become the first African American to play Major League Baseball since Moses Fleetwood Walker in 1884. I was an avid Dodger fan prior to 1947, and I followed the team that year to a National League Championship. I was broken hearted when they lost to the Yankees.

On April 18, 1947, Nancy wrote in her diary that she saw *The Jolson Story* at the Majestic Theater. "It was wonderful," she noted. I was so inspired by Al Jolson's extraordinary voice that for the next fifty years I did impressions of the man some called, "The Greatest Entertainer of the Twentieth Century."

The musical *Jolson* opened in London in 1995 at the Victoria Palace and ran for seventeen weeks. In 1997, Nancy and I were delighted to see Jolson at a theater in Toronto, Canada in box seats right next to the stage. Unfortunately, we could never find evidence the show ever ran on Broadway.

Both Nancy and I were members of the school choir and chorus which performed at the Annual Music Festival on May 9, 1947. We were also members of the youth choir at the Reformed Church where we worshipped regularly and where we were married in 1953.

THE SUMMER OF 1947

When Nancy and I were growing up in Gettysburg in the Forties, we loved our summer activities like swimming at the local pool or one of the numerous parks nearby. A favorite of ours for both swimming and picnicking was Caledonia State Park, 18 miles west of Gettysburg. According to news reports in the summer of 1947, Caledonia was officially recognized by Pennsylvanians as its number one State Park.

Yes, the water was always cold, but the setting and the access to forested picnic areas, made a summer visit to Caledonia enjoyable and memorable.

Over the years, members of our family have continued to visit Caledonia. As recently as this past summer, our daughter and her husband camped at this very popular State Park.

Laurel and Fuller Lakes, about 18 miles north of Gettysburg, were also popular. Nestled in the forests of Pine Grove Furnace State Park, the water was just as cold as Caledonia but we still remember those lakes fondly.

Nancy learned to swim in another popular location a few miles south of Gettysburg called Natural Dam where her parents rented a cottage for family and friends for several summers.

In the summer of 1947, I was a member of the staff at Camp Nawakwa, a Lutheran Leadership Training Camp in Brysonia thirteen miles north of Gettysburg. The Camp had a large pool that was mine to enjoy any time I wasn't working. The only downside was, I had to clean it every few weeks.

Also, that summer Nancy was hired as a counter clerk on weekends at Murphy's 5 & 10 on Baltimore Street. It was a job she held until she entered Shippensburg State Teachers' College in the fall of 1949.

MORE ABOUT THE SUMMER OF 1947

In her diary in July of 1947, Nancy mentioned that "Bruce W. is in the hospital." I had fallen on a tree stump working as a member of the ground crew at Camp Nawakwa and bruised my kidney. The following day, Nancy and her mother brought me flowers.

In August, after I was released from the hospital, Nancy wrote, "In Faber's today we saw Bruce W. He looked awful. He wore glasses and he limps a little when he walks." Fortunately, I didn't look too awful. A few months later, Nancy invited me to go to a party with her. Soon, I would be just "Bruce" in Nancy's diary, not "Bruce W."

In July of 1947, an article in the *Gettysburg Times* reported that Ned Burns, from the National Park Service of Chicago, and mural painter Carle Ciampaglia inspected the cyclorama painting of Pickett's Charge displayed in Gettysburg to determine how the famous work by Paul Philippoteaux could be restored.

In the Forties, the 360-degree cylindrical painting was displayed in the Cyclorama located on the east side of Baltimore Street on Cemetery Hill. The 1863 Inn of Gettysburg is now located there.

When our families had visitors who were not familiar with the Battle of Gettysburg, the Cyclorama was often included in our tour. The massive painting was opened to the public in time for the 50th anniversary of the Battle in 1913. Today, the 377 feet long, 42 feet high Gettysburg Cyclorama may be seen in a three-dimensional setting in the Gettysburg National Park Visitor Center.

THE MAROON AND WHITE AND THE FALL OF 1947

When Nancy and I were growing up in Gettysburg in the Forties, our school newspaper was the *Maroon and White*, and it won a first-place honor award in 1947 in competition sponsored by the Quill and Scroll International. The judges called the paper "an enterprise providing worthwhile and exciting experiences for its staff."

The Wednesday, September 17, 1947 issue of the *Maroon and White* had two full pages of girls' and boys' sports including an article about our first football game which we lost to Delone Catholic 25-6.

The team won only three games the previous year, and expectations were high that the 1947 team could improve on that record. I was one of only six lettermen returning to the team.

In a small box on the sports page under the heading, Attention Sports Fans, there was an appeal for suggestions for a name for our teams which were alternately referred to as, "The Little Bullets," the "Junior Bullets" and the "Maroons." A vote sponsored by the Student Council in our senior year finally created the Warriors, the name teams still use today.

The coming attractions at the Majestic Movie Theater were advertised in the same issue of the Maroon and White, and as usual, three different films were offered within a week. Going to the movies at the Majestic or the Strand was a popular pastime in the Forties before television. No wonder Nancy mentions it so often in her diary.

When the 1947-48 academic year opened at Gettysburg High School, enrollment increased over the previous year by nearly one hundred students. As a result, high school enrollment of 660 students set a new record. Today, enrollment at the Gettysburg Area High School exceeds 1,000.

OUR FIRST DATE IN THE FALL OF 1947

In Nancy's 1947 diary, my name is mentioned several times prior to October 24, but with no hint of anything other than a casual relationship. We danced a few times at the Teen Canteen, and we were officers in the sophomore class, an association that was all business.

All that changed on October 24, 1947 when Nancy wrote, *"I asked Bruce to go to Darlene Kennell's party tomorrow night. He said, 'Sure'."*

Apparently, I didn't have to think much about how I would respond to Nancy's invitation. I said, "Sure.," and we had our first date.

A fire was kindled at Darlene's party that chilly night in the fall of 1947, but it would take another six months before it burst into flame.

Matter of fact, after going on a hayride together the following week, we only saw each other socially at school dances.

One month after our first date, Nancy went with girlfriends to the movies and the Teen Canteen. That night, she wrote in her diary:

"Bruce wasn't even there. I don't think I like him anymore."

In October of 1947, an editor for our school newspaper, the *Maroon and White*, asked for students' reactions to how the girls'

162

skirts were going "down, down, down." Our classmate, Bill Eisenhart, offered the most straightforward answer. Bill said, "No, I can't see enough of the leg."

As I recall, that was my thought exactly.

Nancy at sixteen

PRESIDENT LINCOLN AND THE GETTYSBURG ADDRESS

Gettysburg, Pennsylvania, where Nancy and I grew up in the Forties, is famous for the Civil War battle that occurred there in 1863. The village is also widely known, because it was there on November 19 of 1863 that Abraham Lincoln delivered one of the best-known speeches in American History, the Gettysburg Address.

On November 19, 1947, the students at Gettysburg High School were excused early so we could witness the eighty-fourth anniversary celebration of the dedication of the Gettysburg National Cemetery and President Lincoln's enduring speech.

Unfortunately, we remember very little about the occasion with one exception. Claude Rains, the famous English film star who was nominated four times for an Oscar for Best Supporting actor, recited the Gettysburg Address at the ceremony.

Many people who assume that Lincoln delivered his speech with a rich baritone are surprised to learn his voice was high pitched.

In the award-winning movie Lincoln, Daniel Day Lewis did his best to impersonate the sound of that voice as he spoke the Gettysburg Address.

Currently, on November 19 each year, the Gettysburg National Cemetery is rededicated and Lincoln's speech is remembered in the annual Dedication Day ceremonies and Remembrance Day Parade. The parade attracts thousands of spectators and reenactors alike.

The Annual Remembrance Illumination ceremony occurs in the evening on November 19. The ceremony features luminary candles on each of the 3,512 Civil War soldiers' graves, and the names of each of the known deceased are read throughout the evening.

MORE MEMORIES FROM NOVEMBER 1947

An article in the Gettysburg Times on November 10, 1947 reported on the schools and stores that would be closed on Armistice Day, Tuesday, November 11. Few people today will remember a National Holiday called Armistice Day which honored those who died in service to our country during World War I. In 1954, President Eisenhower signed a bill changing Armistice Day to Veterans Day honoring all veterans of all wars.

Another article in the Times on November 10 reported that Secretary of State, George Marshall asked congress for 597 million dollars to be used to rebuild the war-torn countries of Europe. In what became known as The Marshall Plan, eighteen European countries received a total of 12 billion dollars in economic support. The United Kingdom, France and Germany were the largest recipients.

November was also the month that the people of Adams County were asked to donate food and cash for the starving people of Italy and France. Contributions were delivered to the Shetter House on Chambersburg Street then trucked to Harrisburg and placed on the Friendship Train headed to New York City.

In November, the first call went out for basketball candidates for the 1947-48 season at Gettysburg High School. Twenty-seven students responded including three lettermen from last year, Kenny Fair, Bill Eisenhart and myself.

Finally, the Yankees beat the Dodgers in seven games in the first televised World Series, and Jackie Robinson, second baseman for Brooklyn, became the first African American to play in a Series.

DECEMBER 1947 AND 2016 CONNECTED

Two events that took place in the Gettysburg National Cemetery sixty-nine years apart are linked to each other.

On December 11, 1947, the *Gettysburg Times* reported that twenty-eight veterans of World War II were to be re-interred that month in the Gettysburg National Cemetery.

Sixty-nine years later, on December 2, 2016, members of our family, including four great- grandchildren, placed Christmas Wreaths on the graves of World War II veterans in the Gettysburg National Cemetery. Undoubtedly, some of those who were honored in 2016 were laid to rest in 1947.

Family and friends with Christmas wreaths

Nancy and I have been participating in the National Wreath Project sponsored by the Sgt Mac Foundation since 2008, and this year we were accompanied by fifteen family members and friends. We were among approximately 300 volunteers who decorated wreaths and placed 1620 on headstones in the Gettysburg National Cemetery.

On December 20, 1947, the *Times* quoted William Haskel, assistant to the president of the New York Herald Tribune, who called Gettysburg, "a fresh air paradise." Haskell visited Gettysburg the previous week to discuss the Fresh Air Program which placed youngsters from New York City in Gettysburg for a summer visit.

Nancy's 1947 diary suggests that we were busy sophomores at Gettysburg High School in December of that year. We were both members of the high school choir which performed numerous times leading up to Christmas. In addition, we were both involved in sports, and Nancy worked evenings at Murphy's 5 & 10. When did we find time to study?

CHRISTMAS 1947

We loved Christmas in Gettysburg when we were growing up in that famous Civil War town in the Forties. That was long before political correctness, so "Merry Christmas" was still the popular greeting offered and received. We don't remember anyone saying, "Happy Holidays."

Nancy and I were both active in our school choir and chorus, and we sang often for service clubs during the Christmas Season. Our annual Christmas Program at school on December 23 featured the 200 voices of our combined choir and chorus singing selections from The Messiah by Handel.

Popular music on our radio, juke box or record player in December of 1947 included a song by Perry Como that was a big hit. The memorable lyrics read like this:

"Oh, Chi-baba, Chi-baba, Chihuahua,
Enjilava kooka la goomba,
Chi-baba, Chi-baba, Chihuahua,
My bambino go to sleep."

Other songs in the top ten included Ballerina by Vaughn Monroe and That's My Desire by Frankie Laine. Bing Crosby's 1947 recording of White Christmas is the version of that popular song heard most often today.

Music on Broadway featured four of the biggest hit musicals ever produced: *Brigadoon, Finian's Rainbow, Oklahoma* and *Annie Get Your Gun*.

Nancy's best memory of 1947 was her first prom in the spring of that year. I wish I could report that I was her date, but sadly, I wasn't.

My best memories were starting at forward on a very successful Gettysburg High School basketball team and earning letters in football, basketball and track for the second year.

JANUARY 1948

The spring semester of our junior year at Gettysburg High School in 1948 began with impressive wins in basketball over the Alumni and Waynesboro followed by a loss to the perennial Conference Champion Chambersburg. That loss was followed by seven consecutive wins. Things were looking up for a team on which I was a starting forward.

Basketball scores in the Forties were always very low compared to current contests. For example, in the game against Shippensburg on January 13, the opponents only scored two points in the first quarter and only seventeen for the game. No player on either side scored in double figures.

Nancy and I began dating as a couple in 1948, or as we said back then, "We are going steady." In January, however, no one would have predicted that relationship. As a matter of fact, I was dating other girls, and after an evening with girlfriends and several boys, Nancy wrote in her diary on January 2, "Had a good time. I don't care about Bruce."

In 1948 demographers looking into the future suggested, "There is a strong possibility that within a few decades the population in America will reach its maximum size and will begin to decrease."

That year, it was predicted that 163 million people would live in America by the year 2000. Thanks in part to a baby boom, the population passed 163 million by 1955 and soared to over 325 million at present.

In 1948, Robert Heinlein wrote *Space Cadet*, a novel in which people used cellphones. While the technology for mobile phones was around in the Forties it was not until the mid-Eighties that they became widely available.

DANCES WERE FREQUENT AND POPULAR

Nancy's diary for January and February of 1948 reveals that she and her friends often attended dances sponsored by the school, the canteen, the Elks Club and various service clubs.

The senior canteen sponsored by the Gettysburg recreation center was especially popular with older teens. On January 19, for example 260 teenagers attended the canteen at the Gettysburg Hotel Annex, and of course, Nancy was there with her girlfriends.

I believe it was a dance at the canteen when I first realized what a very special girl Nancy was. But more about that in a future chapter.

There were also dances after basketball games on Fridays when the basketball team played at home. The team ended January on a seven-game winning streak before losing to Waynesboro, a team they had beaten handily in early January.

After every dance or home game, it was customary to go uptown and eat. The most popular spots were the Sweetland and the Delecto on the square. The Blue & Gray Bar & Grill is now located in the building that once housed the Sweetland, and we think T&S Clothing is now located where the Delecto existed in the Forties.

BULLYING AND SEXUALITY IN THE FORTIES

Nancy and I recently read a report from the American Psychological Association, suggesting, "40% to 80% of school-age children experience bullying at some point during their school careers." That data prompted us to think about bullies when we were growing up in Gettysburg in the Forties. Neither one of us could recall a single incident involving us or our friends.

A search of the *Gettysburg Times* published from 1945 through June of 1949 when we were in high school revealed only one mention of someone who was a bully. In April of 1947 there was an article about "bullying coaches who help incite crowds to disorder."

Another subject that was never in the news in the Forties was sexuality. If you Google that term today, you will be led to sites where you will find descriptions of seven different types of sexual orientation: heterosexual, homosexual, bisexual, asexual, polysexual, pansexual and transexual.

When we were growing up in Gettysburg in the Forties, Nancy and I only remember an occasional use of the word "homosexual," but we never used any of the other terms, and we never heard anyone else use them. A search for these words in the *Gettysburg Times* while we were in high school got no hits.

Of course, we also use words today like cell phone, Google, Facebook and iTunes which were unheard of in the Forties, but they describe products or services that were created since then. We assume that seven categories of sexuality existed in the Forties. We just never heard of them. We wonder how many know they exist today.

AROUND HER HAIR SHE WORE A RED RIBBON

Readers may recall that our story began when my family moved to Gettysburg in 1942. That year, I entered sixth grade in Lincoln School where Nancy was also a student. Since we began our blog, we have written about our experiences through the years in and out of school. Now we look back at a very important event in our lives that occurred in the winter of 1948.

In the fall of our junior year in high school in 1947, Nancy invited me to accompany her to parties on two successive weekends, and I accepted her invitations. From that time until February 1948, we danced together occasionally, but never dated each other again.

On Saturday, February 21, 1948, all the clerks at Murphy's 5 & 10 where Nancy worked on weekends were asked to wear a red ribbon in their hair. After work, she still wore the ribbon when she met her friends at the Teen Canteen. I was there with my friends.

Something about the way Nancy looked with a ribbon in her hair lit a spark prompting me to look at her again and again with increasing interest. I asked Nancy to dance three times that night. The last time she had her coat on preparing to leave with her friends, when I asked her to join me once more. In her diary that night, Nancy wrote that I held her "real close."

I believe that I fell in love with Nancy that February night at the Teen Canteen shortly after I turned seventeen. Nancy wouldn't be seventeen for another month.

Incidentally, a popular song in February 1948 was *When You Were Sweet Sixteen* by Perry Como. We may have danced to that song that night at the Canteen.

175

OUR SCHOOL NEWSPAPER: THE MAROON AND WHITE

When Nancy and I were students at Gettysburg High School from 1945 until 1949, our school newspaper, the *Maroon and White*, was published every two weeks. It was a remarkable achievement for a small school, especially in light of the fact the paper was 11x7 inches and typically six pages long.

Several factors were responsible for the success of this excellent publication which was free to all students. The experienced advisors, Louise Ramer and Ruth Mundis, gave direction and guidance to a huge staff of nearly sixty students from all four classes. In addition, each issue of the Maroon and White featured numerous display ads from local businesses.

The Wednesday, March 10, 1948 issue of the *Maroon and White* included fifty-six ads, and recently, Nancy and I walked down memory lane as we reviewed them.

Among the most popular places advertised in the school paper were the Majestic Theater which featured three movies plus a newsreel and cartoon each week; the Sweetland and the Delecto where friends gathered after school, sporting events or after leaving the Canteen; and Smitty's Store located on what is now LeFever Street, for snacks, sodas, ice cream and soft drinks.

The sports news in the March 10 issue of the Maroon and White included a wrap-up of our recent very successful basketball season in which the team won seventeen games and lost five.

Senior Kenny Fair, the leading scorer, was first team All-Conference and honorable mention All-State.

The March 10 edition also carried an ad for Adams County Motors, the Ford dealer where Nancy and I bought our first new car, a 1955 Ford Fairlane Town Sedan, the prettiest car we ever owned.

1955 Ford Fairlane

THE COST OF WINNING WWII

When Nancy and I were growing up in Gettysburg in the Forties, the most important event of that decade was World War II which ended on VJ Day, August 15, 1945. By the spring of 1948, our lives had returned to normal, but an article in The Gettysburg Times that year reminded us once again of the cost of that war.

On March 6, the *Times* reported that the bodies of three men from Adams County who were killed in WWII would arrive in the United States in a few days.

T/Sgt. Richard J. Gross of East Berlin was killed in August of 1943 while serving with the Air Force in New Guinea. Pvt. Maurice Small of Gettysburg was 27 when he was killed in action in Normandy on July 13, 1944, and Pvt. George Spertzel of York Springs, was 25 when he was KIA in France on July 31, 1944.

Adams County records indicate that 3,100 men and women served in World War II, and 110 men from the County were among the 419,000 citizens of the United States who lost their lives in that conflict.

Those buried in the Gettysburg National Cemetery are remembered in annual Memorial Day Ceremonies, and each December a Christmas Wreath is placed on the headstones of veterans of World War II as well as others who have served in the armed forces of the United States.

Nancy and I, along with friends and family, are honored to participate in the Christmas Wreath Project each year.

MINSTREL SHOWS AND COACH FORNEY

When Nancy was a sophomore at Gettysburg High School in 1947-48, she faithfully recorded in a diary her activities for each day. On Friday, April 2, 1948, Nancy wrote that she and two friends attended the Lion's Club Minstrel Show in the school auditorium. The show featured club members in blackface performing dances, solos, jokes, comedy skits and music by a sixteen-voice chorus.

Minstrel shows were a form of entertainment developed in the 19th century and were the first theatrical form that was distinctly American.

They were performed by white men in blackface lampooning black culture in America. Al Jolson appeared in blackface in 1927 in *The Jazz Singer*, the first talking motion picture.

As the civil rights movement progressed and gained acceptance, and because of their overt racist references, minstrel performances were ultimately discontinued. Today most people would consider minstrel shows repulsive and offensive.

On April 5, 1948, the local Rotary Club honored the members of the Gettysburg High School basketball team for a very successful season winning seventeen of twenty-two games and scoring 910 points to opponents 752. I was proud to be a contributing member of that team.

In a speech to the Rotarians, Coach George Forney said, "The job of the coach consists principally in telling the boys their faults, and only in that way can improvement be made." It was clear from his comments that Forney left the accolades and applause   to   the   community.

179

JUNIOR PROM 1948: A MOMENT IN TIME

The April 7, 1948 issue of the *Maroon and White*, our Gettysburg High School newspaper, carried a front- page article about April Showers, the Girl Scout's Dance to be held in the school gym on Saturday, April 17.

Although we were together often for school functions and casual meetings at the Teen Canteen, Nancy and I did not date since the previous fall when she invited me to join her for two parties on successive weekends. April Showers would become a major turning point in our relationship, because when I invited her to go to the dance with me, I was elated when she quickly agreed.

Nancy worked at Murphy's 5 & 10 on Baltimore Street on weekends, so we didn't get to the dance until 9:00, but according to her diary, she had a wonderful time. So did I apparently because a few weeks later, she agreed to go with me to the junior Prom on May 15.

Although dinner, tuxedos and limos were not yet popular, the junior Prom was a big deal in 1948 with an orchestra, decorations, corsages and gowns for the girls. We weren't aware of it that night, but our future together would be forever measured by that moment in time.

From that night on, we have been a couple, dating through high school and college until five years later on May 30, 1953, we stood before a congregation of family and friends and pledged our love for all time. This year, we will celebrate our sixty-fifth wedding anniversary.

A NATIONAL HIGH SCHOOL GRADUATION

In the spring of 1948, the National Association of Secondary School Principals chose Gettysburg High School for a singular honor. Commencement exercises on June 1 that year were broadcast coast to coast over a network of Mutual stations of WOR, New York. The ceremony was referred to as the National High School Graduation. The speaker, Dr. David E. Lilienthal, chairman of the Atomic Energy Commission, gave an address titled, Youth in the Atomic Age.

Following World War II which ended after atomic bombs were detonated over Hiroshima and Nagasaki, Japan, Lilienthal was chairman of a committee that advised President Harry Truman on the position of the United States in the Atomic Age.

In his speech to the graduating seniors, Lilienthal was optimistic about future generations living in the Atomic Age "in which there is less suffering, less poverty, less misery."

"The Atomic Age can become an age of mercy, of joy and hope, one of the most blessed periods in all of history," he concluded.

Nancy and I wonder how Dr. Lilienthal would view the current Atomic Age in which there are believed to be 16,3000 nuclear weapons in nine countries including North Korea led by Kim Jong Un, considered one of the world's most dangerous men.

We wonder how optimistic Dr. Lilienthal would have been about the future of the world if he had foreseen a bomb 3,300 times more powerful than those that fell on Japan in 1945?

181

WORLD WAR II DISRUPTS TOURISM

When Nancy and I inform others that we grew up in Gettysburg, they often tell us how much they love and admire our hometown. Some even speak of moving there. Obviously, they fail to comprehend what it's like in a small town sharing the streets and sidewalks with over a million tourists a year.

When we were growing up in Gettysburg in the early Forties during World War II, gas, oil and tires were rationed, and new cars were no longer available. In addition, there was a national speed limit of thirty-five miles per hour.

As a result of the war and rationing, the number of visitors to Gettysburg dropped dramatically from 670,000 in 1941 before the war began to 118,000 during the first year of the conflict. For the residents of Gettysburg who fought tourist traffic during the busy months, it was a pleasant change, but for motels, restaurants and others who depended on the tourism industry, it was a serious problem.

World War II ended in 1945, and by 1948 when Nancy and I were juniors in high school, tourism in our town returned to normal. In an article in the *Gettysburg Times* on May 3, 1948 Dr. J. Walter Colemen, the Gettysburg National Park Superintendent, reported 47,000 visitors toured the Battlefield in April of that year.

Nancy and I wondered how Park visitation in 1948 compared with the current rate, so we checked with Katie Lawhon, Public Affairs Specialist at the Gettysburg National Military Park, and Lawhon reported that in April of 2016 112,850 people explored the Park, and by the end of last year visits totaled well over one million.

CROONERS OF THE FORTIES

Nancy recently discovered a letter from her mother written in 1951 when Nancy was completing the first term of her sophomore year at what is now Shippensburg University. In her opening paragraph, Mother Ogden wrote:

"You'll just love television, Daddy is having just the grandest time. We've had it 2 nights and the house is full of neighbors each night. Our set is really nice, the picture is clear and my, what fun. We laughed our sides sore tonight."

Many people who grew up with television may wonder how we entertained ourselves growing up in the Forties without it. In her diaries from the Forties, Nancy often mentions going to the movies which in those days changed several times each week. Throughout high school, Nancy often walked to the soda shops on or near the square, and once or twice each week she visited the Teen Canteen to dance and play games with friends.

But when she was alone at night, she often mentions listening to music on the radio, and back in the Forties, when she turned her radio on in the evening, the crooners were coming into their own led by Frank Sinatra, the most popular singer in broadcasting history.

A crooner is a male singer with a soft, intimate style, originally made possible by the introduction of microphones. Crooners were popular in the Thirties, but our earliest recollections are from the mid-Forties when we listened, and often danced to their music.

Nancy and I and most of our friends knew the signature songs that identified each of the crooners as well as the lyrics to many of their recordings. Here are a few favorite crooners with their signature songs:

Perry Como — *Prisoner of Love*
Frankie Lane — *That's My Desire*
Vaughn Monroe — *Racing with the Moon*
Dean Martin — *Everybody Loves Somebody Sometime*
Andy Williams — *Moon River*
Bing Crosby — *The Blue of the Night*

CAMP NAWAKWA AND THE SUMMER OF 1948

Since the Junior Prom at our high school on May 15, Nancy and I were together every day at school and often in the evenings as well. Then, on June 2, it was time for me to leave Gettysburg for my summer job at Camp Nawakwa about twelve miles north of town.

In the summer of 1946, I began working at Nawakwa, a Lutheran camp for children, youth and adults nestled in 336 wooded acres of the South Mountains. I lived and worked at the camp each summer for six years initially, on the ground crew but eventually as an assistant to the chef in the camp kitchen.

According to Nancy's diary, on our last night together, I told her that I would not be seeing her again until the 4th of July. I said, "Absence makes the heart grow fonder." Hah! Five days later, I hitched a ride to Gettysburg with the camp truck driver, and Nancy and I enjoyed a brief visit on a Sunday afternoon.

That summer, we began writing letters, an activity that would last throughout college, my early tour in the Marine Corps and a fourteen-month separation when I was ordered to Japan in 1954. We estimate that from that first letter in 1948 until I returned from Japan, we wrote well over a thousand letters to each other.

Remarkably, we still have the very first letter Nancy wrote to me postmarked June 3, 1948. It was a brief summary of her activities for the day ending with, "Love, Nancy." We also have a letter written to me at Camp on July 4, 1949, and ... "What a

185

difference a year made!" Our letters by that time clearly indicated that we were very much in love.

Every summer for the next four years, Nancy and I were apart during the week while I worked and lived at Camp Nawakwa, but typically, we found a way to be together for a Saturday night date.

85TH ANNIVERSARY OF THE BATTLE

1948 marked the 85th anniversary of the Battle of Gettysburg, so we assumed there would be some recognition of that milestone. Unfortunately, that was not the case.

The *Gettysburg Times* carried stories about the anniversary of the Dubois, Pennsylvania's fire company and the 25th anniversary of Yankee Stadium. Obviously, there were also many reports about local residents celebrating wedding anniversaries, but we found only one reference to the 85th anniversary of the battle. It was a poem by Osborn F. Hevener and published in the *Times* on July 3, 1948.

To Gettysburg
85 Years After

Where Kemper bled and Armistead,
Tall grows the wheat and lush the corn,
Hear I the call of Longstreet's voice,
And rebel yells reborn.
Is Pickett there, in fantasy,
To lead his men to death and glory?
Do waving stalks of flowering grain,
Spring from the soil to tell a story?
And is that tale, terse and unadorned,
A sonnet sure to make one pause:
"Blow wheat, rise corn, caress the meadow,
We who died knew no Lost Cause."

A MEMORABLE DATE IN 1948

On one of our most memorable dates in the summer of 1948, Nancy and I traveled to Hershey Park in Hershey, Pennsylvania. Today, you can drive from Gettysburg to Hershey in less than an hour, but back in 1948 there were very few four lane highways and the trip took much longer.

In the Forties, Hershey Park was one of the most popular and entertaining amusement parks in the northeast featuring a roller coaster, bumper cars, a merry go round and numerous other rides for kids and adults. My favorite park attraction was the penny arcade, a Forties version of a video game paradise. The arcade was filled with dozens of game machines testing your strength, skill and patience or predicting your future and even judging your personality.

Nancy and I always enjoyed a walk through the Hershey Zoo followed by a rest in the shade of the beautifully landscaped Sunken Garden. On a warm day, visitors to the Park could cool off in the swimming pool, before heading to the Ballroom.

On a typical weekend, the featured attraction was in the Hershey Park Ballroom where popular big bands of the Forties entertained their fans.

In our most memorable visit to the Ballroom, we danced to the music of the Tex Beneke Orchestra. Beneke led the Glenn Miller Band until 1950. In 1948, Nancy and I danced to songs that would remain our favorites for the rest of our lives:

Moonlight Serenade, In the Mood, String of Pearls and *Long Ago and Far Away*.

It was a romantic, never-to-be-forgotten evening.

The cars we drove in 1948 didn't have bucket seats or safety belts, and typically, I drove with my left hand on the wheel and my right arm around Nancy who was snuggled up against me. I'm certain that's how we motored back to Gettysburg that night. Undoubtedly, there were a few stops on the trip so we could talk about our enjoyable day at Hershey Park.

THUMBING A RIDE

On July 17, 1948, Nancy wrote in her diary: *"Bruce and another guy are going to Washington. They're hitchhiking and coming home tomorrow."*

Apparently, my friend and I were confident about getting rides from Gettysburg, because according to the diary, we didn't start "thumbing" until late afternoon. Washington is more than eighty miles south of Gettysburg, and a good two hours away by car.

Unfortunately, my only memory of our brief adventure is standing in line to pay our respects to General John Pershing lying in state in the Capitol Rotunda. After several hours we passed the General in five seconds.

General Pershing was famous for commanding the American troops in World War I (1917-1918). Pershing was a hero back then, but modern historians criticize his use of frontal assaults resulting in unnecessarily high American casualties.

According to Nancy's diary, my friend and I had trouble getting a ride back to Gettysburg the following day, so we took a bus from Frederick and traveled the same route Reynolds First Corps and Howard's Eleventh Corps marched eighty-five years earlier prior to the Battle of Gettysburg.

I hitchhiked successfully and often when I was a college student in Lancaster, Pennsylvania fifty miles east of Gettysburg, but my biggest challenge using my thumb to travel was a 450-mile hike from Jacksonville, N.C. to Gettysburg in 1953. In all such cases I was motivated by my desire to be with Nancy.

BANDS AT THE BATTLE OF GETTYSBURG

July 1 to July 3, 1948, marked the 85th Anniversary of the historically significant Battle of Gettysburg. Nancy and I searched her diaries and local newspapers from 1948 to learn how that important date was acknowledged in Gettysburg. Strangely, we found nothing.

In our search, however, we discovered a reference to Guy Allison, a reporter from Glendale, California who claimed that a Confederate brass band played polkas and waltzes to inspire the troops during Pickett's Charge. We should have been skeptical. What troops would be inspired to go into battle listening to waltzes?

According to an article by Logan Tapscott in *The Gettysburg Compiler*, 10 regimental bands entertained and inspired both Union and Confederate troops at various times during the three-day battle, but Tapscott offered no evidence that a brass band was playing before or during Pickett's Charge.

Musicians were often pacifists who cared for the wounded in addition to performing their duties in the band. In reality, band members were much too busy treating the wounded and assisting the surgeons to play, but according to the article in the Compiler the 11th North Carolina band was ordered to perform during the fighting on the McPherson's Ridge on July 2nd.

When Nancy and I were growing up in Gettysburg and on many occasions since, we have visited Bloody Angle on the Battlefield and imagined Pickett's Charge when over 12,000 Confederate

191

troops marched proudly and bravely toward Cemetery Ridge in formation with flags flying.

We never imagined a band playing as Pickett's Charge unfolded. Now, based on the *Compiler* article, we feel certain none existed.

LINCOLN STAMP AND THE NEW SCHOOL YEAR

Early in July 1948, the Gettysburg National Park Service reported that tourist travel from October 1, 1947 to the end of June 1948 exceeded visitations during the same period a year earlier by 25,000 visitors. Tourism in Gettysburg during World War II dropped dramatically, but as of 1948, it was back on track and would shortly break all previous records.

The big front-page news during the summer of 1948 was President Harry Truman's authorization of a stamp to commemorate the 85th anniversary of Lincoln's Gettysburg Address. The new stamp was scheduled to go on sale on November 19, the date of Lincoln's immortal words, known by some as the "greatest speech in the world."

Stamp honors Lincoln's Address

On July 28, 1948, 40 Gettysburg High School students attended a meeting to discuss plans for the coming football season. Ten others who were invited were either working or on vacation.

That was an excellent turnout compared with previous seasons which resulted in losing records.

The following month, 30 of the most promising candidates traveled 25 minutes north of Gettysburg to attend football camp at Camp Nawakwa for ten days. A busy training schedule and a lot of rough work prepared us for the coming season which started on Friday, September 10.

Our senior year began on Wednesday, September 8, 1948, and according to Nancy's diary, we were together in English, Chemistry and Spanish classes. After being apart for much of the summer while I was at Camp Nawakwa, Nancy and I enjoyed each other's company in classes during the week and dating on most weekends.

PENNSYLVANIA BLUE LAWS

When Nancy and I were growing up in Gettysburg in the Forties, we couldn't go to the movies or shop for groceries or clothing on Sundays. Our parents couldn't buy beer or liquor and couldn't buy a car. That's because the Blue Laws, enacted almost 100 years before Pennsylvania became a state, were the law.

In brief, the Sunday Blue Laws prohibited citizens of the State from "working or participating in any sport or diversion." Until 1933, that included professional baseball and football games which we enjoyed on the radio until the early Fifties when we were able to watch Pennsylvania teams on TV.

Blue Laws were intended to force State residents to observe Sunday as a "day of rest," but over the years so many statutes were enacted, revised or repealed that they became unenforceable.

When Nancy and I were growing up, our parents could only buy alcohol and wine in a State owned and operated liquor store, and there was only one in town. To make a purchase, customers placed their order with a clerk who disappeared briefly and returned with your order. Everything was numbered, so if you couldn't pronounce Gewurztraminer, you asked for it by number. "I'll have a bottle of 246."

The legal age for purchasing liquor or an alcoholic drink in a restaurant was, and still is 21, but Nancy and I had our first cocktail when we were 18 on Christmas Eve in 1949. Nancy's Dad made Manhattans for us, and I still use his unconventional recipe today.

195

FALL 1948

Nancy's diaries written in the fall of 1948 indicate that her days were primarily devoted to her studies, work (Murphy's 5 & 10), dating and enjoying her friends. I was involved in football (end), student council (president), dating and not enough with my studies.

By the middle of October, our football team won two, lost two and tied one, scoring 109 points to our opponents 34. We were still contenders for the Conference title, because one of our losses was to a non-Conference team. For the first time in many years, our football team was respected by our opponents.

Because Nancy and I were preparing for college, we were required to enroll in three sciences prior to graduation. Nancy chose science, biology and chemistry. I enrolled in science, physics and chemistry. Both of us had no problem fulfilling the requirement until we took chemistry. Each of us considered chemistry our most difficult subject ... and the most useless.

Saturday night dates at the movies or the Teen Canteen followed by a snack at the Sweetland or Bankerts were a regular part of our routine.

Both of us went to Sunday services regularly at the Reformed Church which served as a hospital during the Battle of Gettysburg and where we would eventually marry on May 30, 1953.

Life was good to us when we were dating in high school. Because of our beautiful family, it's even better today.

Bruce's favorite photo of Nancy in high school

A VERY SPECIAL DAY IN GETTYSBURG

The celebration of the 85th anniversary of the dedication of the Gettysburg National Cemetery began early in the morning of November 19, 1948. That was the day the Lincoln-Gettysburg three- cent commemorative stamp, authorized by President Truman, went on sale at our local post office.

Nancy and I were seniors in high school on that memorable day, and we distinctly remember participating in several of the activities scheduled for the event.

Monument honors Lincoln's Address

For example, I bought several stamps at the post office and an equal number of first day covers from one of the many vendors present for the occasion. Then, after addressing the envelopes to myself, I dropped them in the mail so they would be stamped FIRST DAY OF ISSUE on November 19, 1948. Later, I sold those stamped envelopes to a collector for a nice profit.

According to reports, more than 50 postal employees worked in the basement of the post office all week prior to November 19 processing hundreds of thousands of requests for stamps and first day covers from collectors all over the world. The stamp and cover are still for sale on eBay.

Coincidentally, the actual document that President Lincoln held in his hand on November 19, 1863, returned to Gettysburg on November 19, 1948 and was displayed on the Freedom Train which arrived the previous day. That treasured document was obviously one of the main attractions for the thousands of people who passed through the train.

THE FREEDOM TRAIN

Nancy and I were seniors in high school on November 19, 1948, the day the Gettysburg Address was returned to the place where it was delivered by President Abraham Lincoln 85 years earlier.

The document, reported to have been the copy held by Lincoln when he delivered his famous speech, arrived in Gettysburg on the Freedom Train. A parade of red, white and blue railroad cars carried exhibits of 127 priceless American treasures on a tour of the entire country. In over 300 cities where the train stopped, a rededication week of public celebrations of the United States was scheduled.

In addition to Lincoln's Gettysburg Address, the train carried the original United States Constitution, the Declaration of Independence, Truman Doctrine, the Bill of Rights and many other national treasures. Each historic document was displayed in a beautifully designed protective case highlighted by indirect lighting.

Despite heavy rain, 7,685 persons visited the Freedom Train on the 19th. Nancy's diary notes that it took her an hour to go through all the cars. She also commented on the Marine guards in every car. Four years later, Nancy married her very own Marine. Sixty-five years later he's still hers.

In addition to the visit by the Freedom Train, Rededication Week in Gettysburg included the issue of a special commemorative stamp honoring Lincoln's Address, and a patriotic program in the Majestic Theater which was broadcast all over the country on the Mutual Broadcasting System.

Schools were dismissed early that morning so we could attend the program.

Photo courtesy of Library of Congress
Freedom Train

1948 FOOTBALL SEASON WRAP-UP

The October 23, 1948 Gettysburg High School football game with arch-rival Chambersburg was emblematic of our entire season. We were so close to having a winning game/season, but no trophy.

With four minutes remaining in the game, we were beating the annual Conference champions 13-0. Then we took a nap. Two quick scores on errors by both our offense and defense, and Chambersburg fans left Gettysburg blowing car horns all the way out of town.

I will never get over the disappointment of losing that game, but that night I buried my distress cuddled up to Nancy on a hayride with friends. Now that's a very pleasant memory.

When the season ended, we had won four, lost four and tied one. What the won and loss record did not show was that we outscored our opponents 160 to 60 and we lost three games by a total of 12 points. Considering the losing records of recent football teams, it was an improvement.

The two games we lost by one point were the result of failed extra point attempts by drop kicking which involves dropping the ball and kicking it when it bounced off the ground. The drop kick is no longer used in football, and based on personal experience, that's a good thing.

When the All-South Conference team was announced, Bob Hottle and I were both on the first team, and I was pleased to be selected by our players as the Honorary Captain.

Now that football was over, it was time to prepare for basketball season. With four returning lettermen, hopes were high for another winning season.

GIRLS' SPORTS IN THE FORTIES

Nancy's high school diaries from the Forties are a major source of information for Growing Up in Gettysburg, and in the fall of 1948, she often mentions the Girls' Athletic Association (GAA). While the boys played interscholastic sports, athletic competition for girls was provided through participation in the GAA which offered intramural sports in field hockey, basketball and volleyball. Nancy was involved in all three.

Fifty-one percent of the girls in our senior class at Gettysburg High School participated in GAA-sponsored sports. Today the percent of high school girls across the country participating in all sports is the same.

Currently, there is a total of more than fifty different sports offered to girls in high schools. Basketball is the favorite, and it was the most popular girls' sport back in the Forties. It was also Nancy's preference.

The *Gettysburg Times* archives also provide information for this column, and a front-page story in October 1948 reported that 640,048 tourists visited the Gettysburg National Park from October 1, 1947 to September 30, 1948. The record prior to 1948 was set in 1938 when 1,554,234 tourists visited the Park for the 75th anniversary of the Battle.

Today, the Park welcomes well over a million visitors each year. Back in the Forties, cars were permitted on the Battlefield after dark. Nancy and I took advantage of that often, and we suppose we were counted as tourists.

204

Nancy in her senior year

THANKSGIVING 1948

In an earlier chapter, we reported that President Harry Truman authorized a 3-cent postage stamp to commemorate the 85th anniversary of Lincoln's Gettysburg Address. The stamp went on sale in Gettysburg on November 19, 1948, and shortly before noon on November 24, Postmaster Lawrence E. Oyler announced that total sale of stamps reached 1,123,277. Amazing!

Thanksgiving Eve dances were scheduled throughout Gettysburg on Wednesday, November 24, 1948. The Girls' Athletic Association at Gettysburg High School sponsored the Blue Jean Jump in the new gym, and Nancy and I were there with friends. We never missed a dance at school in our senior year. Nancy's diary notes for that evening suggest we had a good time, as usual.

The Gettysburg Times on November 24 advertised Thanksgiving Day Dinners for unbelievable prices compared to today. The cheapest were Bankerts and the Blue Parrot where a full Thanksgiving dinner was available for $1.25. The Battlefield Hotel at the corner of Baltimore Street and Steinwehr Avenue, asked $2.00, and the Gettysburg Hotel didn't advertise a price. If you have to ask, you can't afford it.

Despite four lettermen on the Gettysburg High School basketball team, by Thanksgiving break we lost a game to Delone and two games to York. We were still optimistic as Conference games didn't begin until January 4.

Looking back on Thanksgiving 1948, Nancy and I are thankful that we found each other when we were so young. Seventy years later, we are still happy to be together and still very much in love.

GETTYSBURG IN RICH FARM COUNTRY

When Nancy and I were growing up in Gettysburg in the Forties, many of our friends at Gettysburg High School were members of the Future Farmers of America (FFA). Reports in the school newspaper and the *Gettysburg Times* revealed our fellow students were active in the FFA in Adams and Franklin Counties and in the State as well.

In our senior year, eighty members of the Gettysburg Chapter of the FFA participated in the Farm Show in Harrisburg where three GHS students won State-wide honors.

Many visitors to Gettysburg who come to study the battle, may not realize that our famous town is located in some of the richest farm and orchard country in Pennsylvania. From the town square, you can drive in any direction and you will immediately realize that farming drives the local economy.

North of Gettysburg, in the South Mountain Fruit Belt, there are 20,000 acres of fruit orchards, and when I was a teenager, I picked cherries in the late spring and peaches in the summer.

Today, the Adams County Fruit Growers organize the annual Apple Blossom Festival in early May of each year. In 2017, the 62nd Festival was celebrated with a full schedule of entertainment at the South Mountain Fair Grounds in Biglerville north of Gettysburg.

On July 1, 2 and 3, 1863, many of the farms surrounding Gettysburg were the scene of some of the bloodiest fighting in the Civil War. The fact is that the battle is named for the town, but most of the fighting took place in the farm fields and woods surrounding Gettysburg.

CHRISTMAS 1948

Nancy and I enjoyed our first Christmas together in 1948. How could we possibly know that sixty-nine years later we would return to Gettysburg with thirteen family members and eight friends to participate in the Christmas Wreath Project in the National Cemetery.

Christmas in Gettysburg in 1948 was synonymous with American values at the time. Political Correctness was not yet a concept, and our school choir sang carols all over town, window displays featured scenes from the Nativity and friends and strangers wished each other Merry Christmas when meeting on the street.

Early in December, Nancy was appointed chairman of a school committee to order and distribute name cards for seniors, a tradition that apparently continues to this day. We collected cards from everyone in the graduating class and placed them in a book we lost long ago.

At a Christmas Dance following a basketball game on Friday, December 23, we danced to *Buttons and Bows* by Dinah Shore, *A Tree in the Meadow* by Margaret Whiting and *Nature Boy* by Nat King Cole. The latter was so slow, we could fall asleep dancing before the song was over.

On Broadway, the musical *Kiss Me Kate* opened just after Christmas and ran for 1,077 performances in New York City. The following year, it won the first Tony Award presented for Best Musical, and sixty-nine years later, Nancy and I attended a performance of the musical presented by our local theater group. We call that durable.

GETTYSBURG WARRIORS ARE BORN

When Nancy and I were seniors at Gettysburg High School in 1948-49, we were involved in what was the most durable decision made by the student body at that time.

The high school colors were and still are maroon and white and prior to February 10, 1949, sports writers referred to our football, basketball, baseball and track teams as the "Maroons." Before 1945, teams were occasionally referred to as Little Bullets, a nod to Gettysburg College teams called the Bullets.

Early in 1949, members of the high school student council decided it was time to select a name for our teams chosen by the students and not the sports writers. The student body was canvassed for suggestions, and among the names mentioned were Warriors, Little Bullets, Picketeers, Lancers, Owls, Rams, Minute Men and Buccaneers.

The names suggested most often were placed on a ballot and on Thursday, February 10 during club period, the name Warriors won by a student body vote of 257 over the Cannoneers which was second with 178 votes. The new name was used by the media for the first time when the Gettysburg Times reported our win over the Mechanicsburg basketball team on February 15: Warriors Lace Mechanicsburg 44-26 in the South Penn Contest.

In 1949, four Gettysburg High School teams were referred to as Warriors. Today there are six boys teams and six girls teams. That's progress, but the name remains the same.

DATING, CHURCH AND BASKETBALL

In our senior year at Gettysburg High School, Nancy and I were together often on Friday and Saturday nights. A typical Friday night date began after a football game or a basketball game followed by dancing in the school gym, the Teen Canteen or Woodlawn.

Our dates usually ended with a late-night treat at the Sweetland, the Delecto, Bankert's, Smitty's, Weaner's or one of the other places catering to hungry teenagers.

A memorable date in our senior year was the Valentine's Day Dance at the Gettysburg Country Club. The love we expressed for each other that night gave us confidence in a future together. I usually left Nancy on weekend dates at midnight, but that night I didn't leave until 2:00 a.m.

Despite keeping late hours on Saturday nights, we regularly went to church on Sunday mornings to the Evangelical and Reformed Church on the corner of South Stratton and East High Streets. Today, it is known as Trinity United Church of Christ.

Nancy and I were both confirmed in the Reformed Church where we were active on committees and the adult choir. In 1953, after dating for five years, Nancy and I were married in that church.

The end of February marked the completion of boys' basketball season with a final record of ten wins and ten losses. It was a disappointing record considering the depth of experience on the squad. Our center, Guy Donaldson, was chosen for the All-Conference Team, and I led the team in scoring when the season ended.

FAMOUS VISITORS AND A SPECIAL GUIDE

An article in the Gettysburg Times on Saturday, March 5, 1949, included the names of famous people who visited the historic town. The list was compiled by Dr. Charles H. Huber, the former director of the women's division of Gettysburg College.*

Among those mentioned in Dr. Huber's memoir were the Count of Paris, the Queen of Hawaii and Teddy Roosevelt who apparently attracted larger crowds than those who gathered in Gettysburg to welcome Abraham Lincoln in 1863.

According to documents from the Adams County Historical Society, sixteen presidents have visited Gettysburg while they were in office. One of those presidents was Jack Kennedy, and his guide for that visit was Col. Jacob "Met" Sheads.

Col. Sheads was a popular history teacher when Nancy and I were students at Gettysburg High School from 1945 to 1949.

Sheads was a battlefield guide during the summer, and it was common knowledge that he knew more about the battle than anyone else. Undoubtedly, that's why he was chosen to be the guide for President Jack Kennedy when he toured the battlefield on March 31, 1963.

It is reported that Col. Sheads suggested that Kennedy return to Gettysburg on November 19 for the 100th anniversary of Lincoln's Address. Kennedy responded, "I'd like to, but I can't. I have to go to Dallas and mend fences." President John F.

Kennedy was assassinated in Dallas on Friday, November 22, 1963.

*Dr. Huber was the Headmaster of the Gettysburg Academy in 1921 when Nancy's mother, Grace Mae Hartman was a senior there. Dr. Huber also served as president of the Gettysburg National Bank where Nancy's father worked for forty-six years.

TEAM PARTY AND THE NATIONAL CEMETERY

In the spring of 1949, the basketball season was over for the Gettysburg High School JV and Varsity teams and also for the Girls' Athletic Association as well. Nancy was one of the leading scorers on her GAA championship team.

After the Varsity boys' season ended, Nancy and I attended a party at the home of senior team member, Bill Eisenhart. Nancy's diary reveals that a few boys drank beer, but most drank cokes. No one drank hard liquor, and no one used drugs.

Matter of fact, in 1949 we weren't familiar with recreational drugs except perhaps for marijuana, and no one we knew used it.

A front-page story in the April 4,1949 issue of the *Gettysburg Times* reported the bodies of two men who served in World War II were to be reinterred in the Gettysburg National Cemetery. Pfc. William O'Neill, of McKeesport and S1C Joseph Coradetti of Wilkes-Barre were originally buried in American cemeteries abroad.

In 2010, there were 1,624 WWII veterans buried in Gettysburg, including Marine Pvt. Paul Heller who was killed in action on October 8, 1942 at Guadalcanal at the shocking age of fifteen. Heller is probably the youngest serviceman buried in the National Cemetery outside of the Civil War section.

My Uncle, Herman "Bud" Houck who served with the U.S. Army in the South Pacific in WWII, is buried in the Gettysburg National Cemetery, and each year in December members of our family place a Christmas wreath on his headstone.

SEGREGATION IN GETTYSBURG IN 1949

The last few months of our senior year at Gettysburg High School in the spring of 1949 were filled with baseball games, track meets, final exams, a Student Council Conference hosted by our school, an Easter music program, dances and a senior prom.

One of the most memorable events was our class trip to Washington on April 25 and 26. We left school early Monday morning and toured all the major sites and returned to Gettysburg late Tuesday. Monday night the girls checked in at the Cairo Hotel and the boys stayed at the Martinique.

Nancy's diary for that trip reveals a forgotten and troublesome memory. According to Nancy, our seven black classmates did not join us. That information prompted me to call our classmate Betty Lee Dorsey Myers who still lives in Gettysburg.

Betty Lee confirmed Nancy's notes and revealed the reason they didn't go was because they knew they would not be welcome in Washington.

Then Betty Lee also revealed that when we were in Gettysburg High School in the Forties, she and her black friends were never welcome at the places we frequented including the Teen Canteen. Nancy and I were dumbfounded. How could there have been such racial discrimination, and we were not aware of it? Or were we simply naive? Nearly seventy years later, we are both embarrassed and ashamed.

Betty Lee also informed me that she is a former elementary school teacher in Gettysburg who graduated from Shippensburg University. She is also the author of *Segregation in Death: Gettysburg's Lincoln Cemetery*.

Incidentally, Betty Lee prefers to be recognized as a "black" woman which is why she was described as such here.

THRILL OF VICTORY: AGONY OF DEFEAT

In my scrapbook of faded news clippings, readers will find an account of my participation in sports from seventh grade at Lincoln School through our senior year at Gettysburg High School. From the beginning to the end, it is a record of "the thrill of victory and the agony of defeat."

One of the thrills in our senior year included my selection as a member of the first team on the South Penn All-Conference football squad. In addition, I was the leading scorer on the squad and a member of the second team All-Conference squad in basketball.

In track, I continued winning the 110 low hurdles, setting a new school and conference record which will never be broken. That's because that race was replaced by the 200-yard low hurdles in the Fifties and Sixties.

The first time I ran the 180-yard low hurdles was at the District meet in Lancaster. I won that race and that qualified me for the State competition at Penn State University.

After winning my heat in the preliminaries, I ran in the finals and fell, something I never did in any other race in my high school career. That incident truly best represents the agony of defeat in my career in sports.

When I returned to Gettysburg that night, Nancy was waiting for me. In her diary for that day she wrote, "He was kind of blue at first, but he soon got over it and we had a good time.

The thrill of victory, the agony of defeat and the joy found in a loving relationship.

Nancy at seventeen

GRADUATION AND SEPARATION

The closer Nancy and I got to graduation from Gettysburg High School in the spring of 1949, the busier we were. Preparing for finals was a chore, especially in courses like chemistry, a subject we never used the rest of our lives. What a complete waste of our time and energy.

Swanee Serenade, our senior dance, was a very special event in our lives. Nancy wore a new yellow gown, and I wore a new suit. Unlike proms today, there was no limousine, no restaurant dinner, no tuxes and unfortunately, no photographs to remind us of this special occasion in our young lives.

On May 30, we stood in front of Nancy's home on Baltimore Street, and with a crowd of over 5,000 people, we watched one of the best Memorial Day parades held in Gettysburg in a long time. As we watched the children walk by with flowers for the graves in the National Cemetery, we were reminded of our participation in this annual event.

Graduation was painful because it meant we would no longer see each other every day. In the fall, Nancy would attend Shippensburg State College, and I accepted a football scholarship to attend Franklin and Marshall College in Lancaster, PA. We would be 86 miles apart, and we were concerned about staying together as a couple.

We knew the separation would be stressful, but we kept in touch with letters and an occasional visit on a weekend, and we made it. On May 30, 1953 we were married, and sixty-five years later, our twin sons, our daughter, eight grandchildren and five great-grandchildren are living proof that "love conquers all."

Senior Pictures

FROM HIGH SCHOOL SWEETHEARTS TO ADULT PARTNERS

In 1949, Nancy and I reached a turning point in our relationship. We were no longer high school sweethearts who saw each other every day and dated almost every weekend. 1949 would always be the year we graduated from high school sweethearts to serious adults planning to spend a life together as husband and wife enjoying a family.

Nancy and Bruce with sons, Steve and
Doug and daughter Tammy

In memory of that important year in our lives, we referred to the Pages of Time for other events which occurred that year.

Harry Truman was our president in 1949 when the average income was just under $3,000 and average price of a new car cost $1,400. Today the mean income is around $35,000, and the typical price for a new car is $33,560.

Life expectancy when Nancy and I graduated was 63 years. Today, we are expected to live to be 79 years old.

When my Dad stopped at the Gulf station for gas, he would often ask for, "A buck's worth." For a dollar in 1949, he got almost six gallons. Today, for the same amount of gas, we pay an average of $15.18.

When we rode our bikes to the corner "Mom and Pop" grocery store for a gallon of milk and a loaf of bread, we paid $.84 for the milk and $.14 for the bread. Today, the milk cost $3.50 and the bread cost $2.59.

Finally, if Nancy and I had purchased one share of Pepsi Cola Stock in 1949 at $9.75 and never withdrew money from it, today, we would have 402 shares because of splits and reinvestments, and the value of our shares would be $45,024. If we had purchased ten shares, today we would have...we don't want to know! As Sinatra sang:

"Regrets we have a few, but then too few to mention."